MINIATURE MAN

Identification & Price Guide

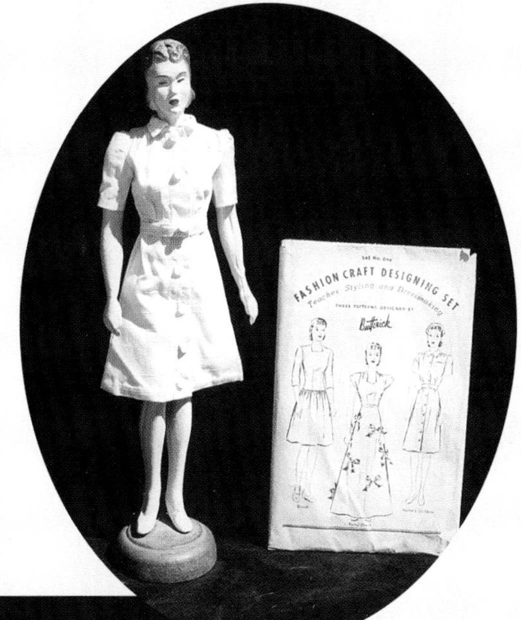

by Doris Mixon

Published by  Hobby House Press
Grantsville, Maryland 21536
www.hobbyhouse.com

Dedication

I would like to dedicate this book to my wonderful husband, Robert, who has been a continuous shoulder to lean on in everything that I do, and with whom I have spent 27 wonderful years. To my two beautiful daughters, Christina, for being there for me constantly even through the tough times, and Leah, my comedian, who keeps me laughing. To my foster mother, Liz Sheldon, who has always believed in me and in whatever I chose to do. To my sister Kim Minnis, for letting me call her and whine constantly, and for being the best sister anyone could have. To Ozzie Mancinelli, a true friend who believed in my talents so much that he hired me as a designer for Paradise Galleries. To Gale Jarvis and Herb Brown who have helped so much in so many ways. To all my doll friends, Harry Klein, David Escobedo, Brian Shafer, Steve Gary, Holly Miner, Doris Smith, Linda Warter, Joe and Jeff, Rae Armellino and Helen Skinner.

Captions Table of Contents: Top to Bottom:
Vintage sewing accessories from the 1940's.

This book was part of a high school library in the 1950's. It encouraged young girls to pursue a career in the fashion industry.

1940's 14in (36cm) display bride mannequin.

Additional copies of this book may be purchased at $24.95 (plus postage and handling) from
Hobby House Press, Inc.
1 Corporate Drive, Grantsville, MD 21536
1-800-554-1447
www.hobbyhouse.com
or from your favorite bookstore or dealer.

Printed in the United States of America

ISBN: 0-87588-597-7

Table of Contents

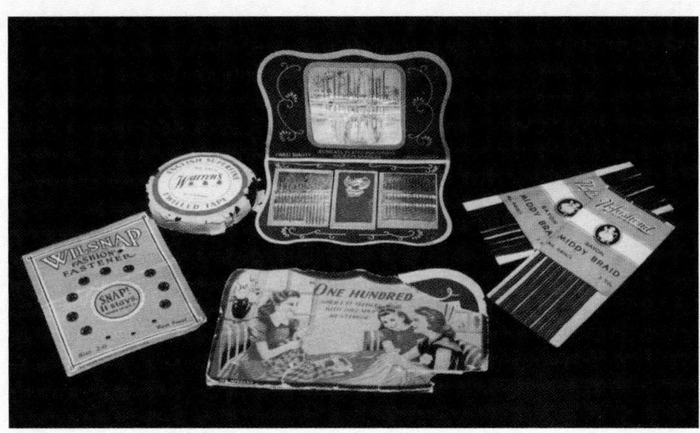

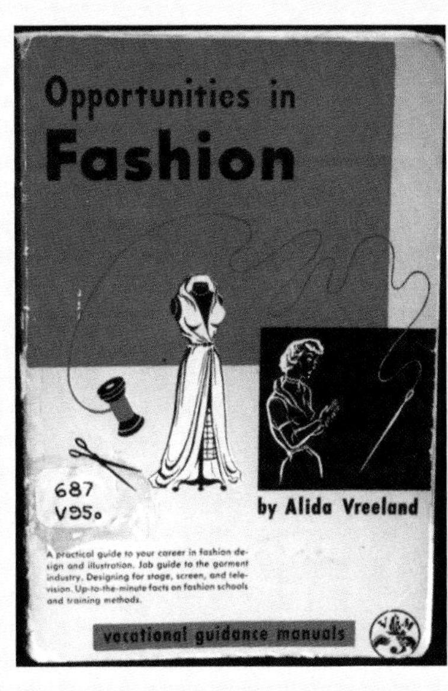

Acknowledgments 4

Introduction 5

Le Theatre de La Mode—(Theater of Fashion) 9

Mel Odom and His Girls 15

Miniature Display Mannequins 17

Mannequin Sewing Dolls 33

Butterick Sewing Kits 39

McCall Sewing Kits 45

Simplicity Sewing Kits 49

Singer Sewing Kits 59

Off-Brand Sewing Kits 63

Caring for Your Miniature Mannequins 79

Mannequin Patterns 85

Mannequins in the Doll World 109

Mannequin Dolls Price Guide 122

Pattern Prices for the Sewing Mannequins 125

About the Author 128

Acknowledgments

I would like to give a special thanks to the following people for their generosity and assistance in putting this book together. Without them this book would not have been possible. First, thanks to Mel Odom, for allowing me to include a picture of Vera and Miami, his wonderful girls, in this book, and for being a great friend and inspiration. Thanks to Laura Meisner, for being such a great source of information while this book was being compiled. To Jim Faraone, who knows what I went through, and for making himself available to be a sounding board. Thanks to Beth Owens, who gave me direction and to Connie and Brent George, for allowing me to use pictures of their beautiful display mannequin and for being great doll friends. Finally, thanks to Debbie Weinstein, a wonderful designer and truly generous soul, for sending me pictures of her great display mannequins and mannequin patterns.

Introduction

During the depression years, when everything was at a premium, sewing was an essential way of life. Then, during the World Wars, sewing was a way to help save material that was sorely needed for the war effort. It was during these bleak times that the display and sewing mannequins became popular items. These mannequins were used to promote sewing and fashion as well as to conserve space and fabric. A regular-size adult outfit could use a precious amount of material while a miniature display mannequin would only require maybe 1/2 yd (.46m) at best. Children were taught to be self-sufficient and thrifty by using sewing kits. Young girls were taught sewing skills at a very young age, and they were given sewing kits with miniature mannequins as a way of making sewing fun. Some of these kits included miniature sewing machines as yet another teaching tool.

When I was a young girl growing up in the 50's and 60's, any proper young lady was expected to know how to cook and sew. Home economics was

A *Good Housekeeping* magazine titled *Teaching Little Girls to Sew*.

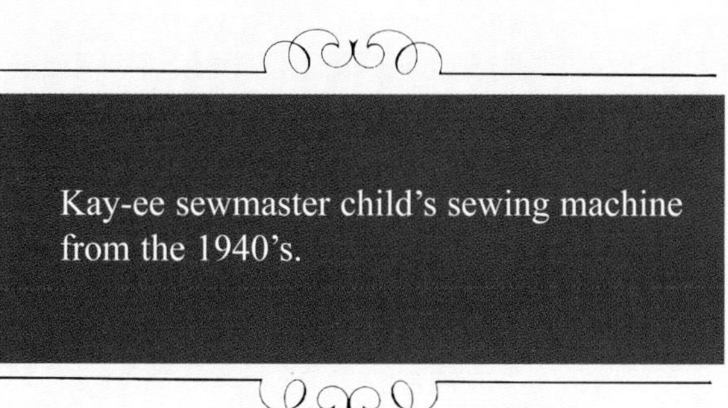
Kay-ee sewmaster child's sewing machine from the 1940's.

Picture puzzle with a young girl learning to sew for her doll on a Singer sewing machine.

a required subject in high school in order to teach a young woman how to take care of a husband and family. In 1962, *Good Housekeeping* also came out with a book called *Teaching Little Girls to Sew*, which included patterns to make simple things such as a bath mit and pot holder. I tried my hand at sewing at a young age. When the Barbie® doll was introduced in the early 1960's, I would take scarves and tie them around her body just to get that perfect fashion statement. I sewed doll dresses by hand out of hankies and old pieces of fabric. I learned how to sew real-people cloths on an old Singer peddle sewing machine. I would spend hours pumping that old machine just to get a few straight lines and my legs would cramp way before I made any significant headway. Finally, I made myself a dress that hung like a potato sack on me, but I made it all by myself and I was proud of it. In today's hurried world, sewing seems to be a thing of the past. Most women work outside of the home to help give their families a better life; therefore, most women don't have the time that is needed to sew for their families. If they are lucky, they might be able to sew on a loose button now and again. If a garment rips, it is most likely thrown out and replaced with a new one. Knitting and crocheting are rarely taught, as is the fine art of tatting (lace making). Therefore, in this book I will take you back to the years when sewing was a necessity and fashion was a matter of what you could dream up.

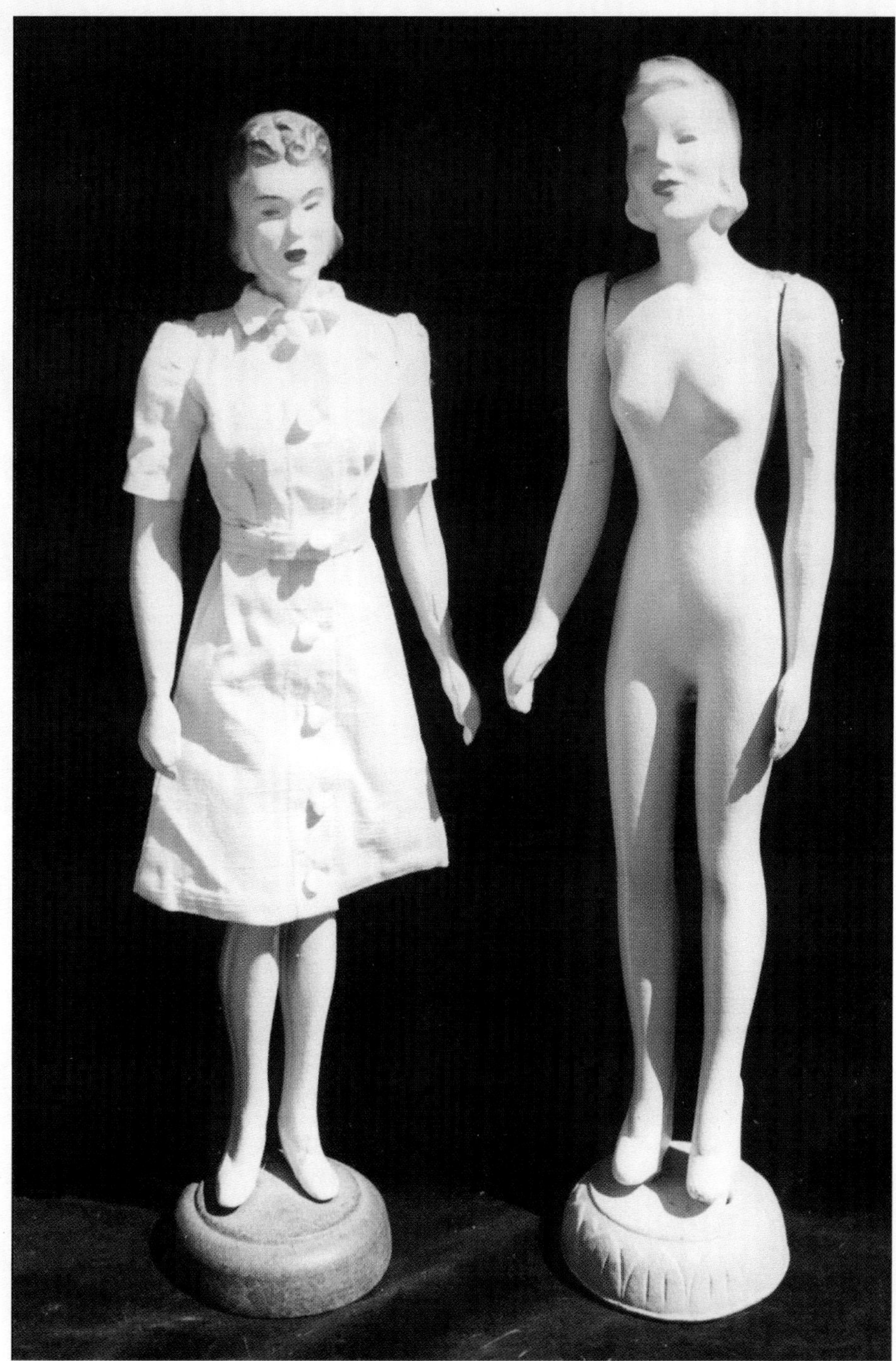

Two *Butterick* child's sewing mannequins from the 1940's.

Simplicity sewing books giving advice for beginners and experts.

I will take you to the era of Le Theatre de la Mode. The fashion houses of Paris rose out of the ashes of World War II to regain their status as the fore runners of haute couture by using miniature wire mannequins to preserve their very limited materials. We will then proceed to the counter display mannequins of the 40's and 50's with their mini variations of human designs, and then into the world of children learning to sew using their own mannequin dolls. We will then take a short look at how the pattern houses of the day designed for fashion mannequins of the time. I hope that this book will impart some valuable information on your quest to find that elusive childhood possession, that perfect miniature mannequin to add to your collection, or just to impart some bits of wisdom on this unique collecting field.

Le Theatre de La Mode—(Theater of Fashion)

Though France was victorious at the end of World War II, it faced a serious economic plight. After being occupied for four years, with every possible commodity in short supply, France was desperate to rebuild its economy, and stimulate production in order to create jobs. With fashion being France's leading industry, it was imperative that this sector reassert itself and support the recovery effort despite the affects of the war. With the Paris costume houses fearful of losing their world status as arbiters of fashion to New York and London, Robert Ricci, son of Nina Ricci, conceived of an idea to both rekindle the French fashion industry and simultaneously raise funds for war relief. Since fabric shortages made it impossible to develop a full-size, human-scale design collection for 1945, Mr. Ricci revived an old costume house tradition of creating collections in miniature. With his being president of the Chambre Syndicale de la Couture, the organization that represents and markets the entire French haute couture industry, he felt that his idea was plausible. So, out of the depths of war and tragedy in France, hope arose in the form

Le Palais-Royal, part of the Theatre de la Mode, by Andre Dignimont. The mannequin wears a navy and white checked twill dress with a fitted bodice and short puff sleeves. The skirt is cut on the bias and has a cummerbund. Her wide rolled-brim hat is made of shiny navy straw with white faille lining. Her elbow-length gloves are made of blue leather.

La Theatre by Christian Berard.

of an army of miniature mannequins. Couturiers, theater artists, artisans, and fashion workers put aside rivalries, scraping and scrounging piecemeal from 1944 to 1945 for the rationed materials needed in this unified statement of defiance and hope. Sculptors such as Jean St. Martin and Elaine Bonabel created one-third human-scale mannequins of a unique wire armature design with non-painted plaster heads.

These were then distributed to the couture houses to be dressed and appointed. Fifty-three designers participated, including such fashion leaders as Baleciaga, Pierre Balmain, Jacques Fath, Madame Gres, Jacques Heim, Hermes, Jeane Lanvin, Lucien Lelong, Nina Ricci, Paquin, Jean Patou, Schiaparelli and the father of haute couture, the House of Worth.

Ma Femme est une Sorciere (My Wife is an Enchantress) by Jean Cocteau for the Theatre de le Mode.

La Grotte Enchantee by Anore Beaurepaire for the Theatre de la Mode. This mannequin wears a raspberry satin long-sleeved evening gown with a tiny collar, narrow sleeves, and a full skirt. Pearls and ruby beads are embroidered on the dress and pillbox hat.

Accessories designers created miniature shoes, handbags, gloves, hats, belts, and umbrellas while famous coiffeurs created elegant hairstyles. The garments and accessories were meticulously crafted as if to be worn by a real woman. The buttons, zippers and buckles all "worked" and the purses opened and originally revealed tiny lipsticks and compacts. Some of the couturiers even dressed their mannequins in lingerie. Jewelers such as Cartier, Van Cleef and Arpels designed beautiful real jewelry to scale.

After the elaborate costuming and accessorizing, the mannequins were then placed in front of twelve miniature theatrical sets designed by top graphic artists of the time.

Christian Berard, an only child of a bourgeois Parisian family, created an opulent Paris Opera scene for mannequins wearing evening gowns. Interestingly, Berard chose the theme of a theater with rows of boxes.

This model from the Theatre de la Mode has a full-length ermine cape lined in pink satin. The matching pink evening gown has a strapless bodice and full skirt embroidered in a scroll design of old gold sequins. Her gloves are made of pink kid skin.

This mannequin is from *Le Palais Royal* by Andre Dignimont. She wears a cap-sleeved dotted turquoise and white chiffon dress with cowl draped bodice. The dress has white organdy collar and cuffs. It has a matching chiffon sash wrapped and tied in a large bow. The hat is natural straw with ivory grosgrain ribbon.

When asked to create a set for the Theatre de la Mode, Jean Cocteau decided to pay homage to the most famous French filmmaker of the period, Rene Clair, using as his inspiration the picture *Ma Femme est une Sorciere (My Wife is an Enchantress)*. Of all the decors designed for the Theatre de la Mode, only Cocteaus's conjures up an image of war or, more generally, of destruction. Cocteau, born into a wealthy Parisian family, crafted a surrealistic Paris garret scene, which depicts Paris' destruction—gaping holes in the walls open to a morose black and white photograph of the city, yet the characters are dressed in elegant ball gowns for a gala evening. Their eyes are fixed on the scene's main character, the sorceress, poised by a bombed out hole in the roof. The present set is a modern replica made following the original documentation.

Andre Dignimont had just finished the décor for the final ballet of Serge Lifar when he began work on his set for the Theatre de la Mode. Philippe d'Orleans built the *Palais Royal*, an ensemble of buildings and archways surrounding a garden, in the late eighteenth century. At the time of the French Revolution and the First Empire, stylish women went to the Palais to purchase elegant new fashions, which they paraded around the garden while exchanging the latest political news and gossip.

Henri Sauget even composed incidental music for the theatre while Boris Kochno, a close associate of Diaghilev's Ballet Russe, provided lighting and choreography.

The Theatre de la Mode first opened at the Pavillon de Marsan in 1946, a wing of the Louvre. It then traveled to London and throughout Europe. After touring Europe, it was sent to New York and other cities in the United States. The last venue was the De Young Museum in San Francisco. At that time, Maryhill Museum had a close relationship with the Fine Arts Museum of San Francisco as the art patroness, Alma de

This Christian Berard mannequin wears an evening gown in white bourdelin crepe and real mink coat. The gown has a draped bodice and string straps. The narrow skirt has front fullness and a network of embroidery of ivory velvet. It has beaded tassels at her hips.

This mannequin features a draped dress in sulfur yellow jersey. The square-necked draped dress has short sleeves and back buttoning. The finely pleated asymmetric draping to the top extends into the full skirt. The dress is accompanied by purple suede belt, hat, gloves, and platform sandals.

Bretteville Spreckels, served as trustee and benefactor of both organizations. It was through this connection that the mannequins were eventually given to the Maryhill Museum, where they have been exhibited since 1952.

After a hiatus that lasted more than three decades, the mannequins returned to Paris in 1988 for rejuvenation, and were then sent out on another world tour blending fashion and history. The mannequins have inspired contemporary designs in both the doll world and fashion world. Today, the Theatre de la Mode consists of 172 mannequins and 9 sets. The 9 original sets were recreated using original drawings created by Ann Surgers, while the mannequins were in Paris from 1988–1990.

The Maryhill Museum of Art, a chateau-like mansion overlooking the Columbia River Gorge, is open 9 to 5 daily, including all holidays, mid-March through mid-November. It is located 100 miles east of Portland, Oregon on the Lewis and Clark Trail, Washington Scenic Route 14. There are over 26 acres of exquisitely landscaped gardens with sculptures and peacocks providing a stunning backdrop for the chateau. Café Maryhill serves gourmet coffee, beverages, deli foods and desserts. The gift shop features original Native American jewelry, books, cards and unique art gifts.

For further information contact: Lee Musgrave (509) 773-3733
Fax (509) 773-6138
E-mail: maryhill@gorge.net

This Jean St. Martin mannequin wears a three quarter-length jacket in raspberry wool jersey over a fitted black wool dress. The jacket features three ceramic buttons, raglan sleeves, and wide black wool cuffs. The dress has a small, notched collar and a black and pink dotted wool sash. Her hat has two black velvet fringed feathers. The outfit is accompanied by black-suede ankle-strap sandal with leather heels.

Mel Odom and His Girls

Awhile back, I was having a phone conversation with Mel Odom, the creator of the Gene Doll, and we got on the subject of mannequin dolls. He told me that he had two display mannequins of his own, Vera and Miami. Well, I was very interested and started asking questions. I naturally wanted to know where he found these dolls. "Well, let's see," he said. "I found Vera in an antique shop in Richmond, VA, in 1971 after a friend told me about seeing her there. Apparently, she had been there for quite awhile. And Miami was given to me by my good friend, Steve Long." Mel also told me a funny story about when he was younger and attending school in Leeds, England. Mel said that he didn't know anyone in England so he took Vera with him so that he would feel a little more at home. His good friend Tim Kennedy had dressed Vera in a beautiful black traveling suit with gold braid and beads and a little pill box hat. When he arrived in England and was going through customs, they checked his luggage and saw this doll. The customs agents got suspicious of an adult man having a doll in his luggage, so they made Mel take her out of his suitcase and undress her right there as well as take off her arms so that they could check for drugs. They stood there shaking Vera and eyeing Mel suspiciously, before they handed her back and told him to proceed. Since he took her with him whenever he went back to the states he ended up having to do this quite a few more times before they recognized him as the crazy American with the doll.

Vera and Miami are 24in (60cm) display mannequins. Vera Valleques is now dressed in a Tim Kennedy original gown of Fortuny fabric, which was a fragment of a vintage garment. He used every quarter inch of the existing material to execute this beautiful interpretation of the classic Fortuny, Delphos gown. Miami was dressed by the brilliant men's wear designer Brian Scott Carr. She wears a creation of stretch jersey and corduroy with a necklace of chains. They both have the same body shape except that Miami is one solid mold whereas Vera has detachable arms. Mel told me that he loves the style and elegance of these miniature ladies and is very happy to have them as houseguests.

These 24 in (61cm) display mannequins are two of the first fashion "dolls" in Mel Odom's collections *Vera Vallequez* is on the right and *Miami* is on the left.

Vera Vallequez (right) is dressed in a fortuny fabric gown created by Tim Kennedy from a fragment of a vintage garment. Tim used every bit of fabric to execute this beautiful interpretation of the classic fortuny Delphos gown. *Miami* (left) wears an original design by the brilliant menswear designer, Brian Scott Carr. Her darker skin tone and jointless arms suggest that she was created for shoulder-baring summer wear.

Miniature Display Mannequins

Miniature mannequins first appeared in recorded history in 1391 when Isabeau of Bavaria, queen of France, sent dolls from France to England to share the newest French fashions. Parisian dolls also were sent as far away as the colonies of the Americas to illustrate the current fashions of Paris. These dolls arrived every four or five months on sailing vessels. Not only did they show the latest French fashions, but they served as dressmaker's models, too. Dressmakers copied the mannequins right down to their hairstyles and accessories. These dolls were exempted from embargoes even during war times. During the European Wars, fashion dolls were so popular that a person carrying them was guaranteed safe passage in war zones. These fashion dolls were treated with high regard knowing that you didn't meddle with women's fashion or you could expect the wrath of your wife or daughter when you got home. So, these early dolls were, in essence, the first miniature fashion mannequins of their time. Sending such dolls to other countries remained popular until the 1700's when such fashion magazines as *The Ladies Magazine*, *The Ladies Monthly Museum*, and *Entertaining Companion for the Fair Sex* were introduced. These magazines gave ladies the fashion updates that they wanted and gradually replaced the fashion dolls.

Mannequins have long been associated with fashion so, the McCall pattern company used that concept to their best advantage in 1939 when they commissioned Margit Nilsen of England to create the first miniature counter display mannequins. These beautiful mannequin dolls were used to display miniature versions of actual

This 5in (13cm) mannequin head was created to display hats. She is from the collection of Debbie Weinstein.

Top to Bottom:
Close-up of bridal display mannequin of the 1950's.

Close-up of a late 1940's display mannequin.

Close-up of a lingerie display mannequin of the 1940's.

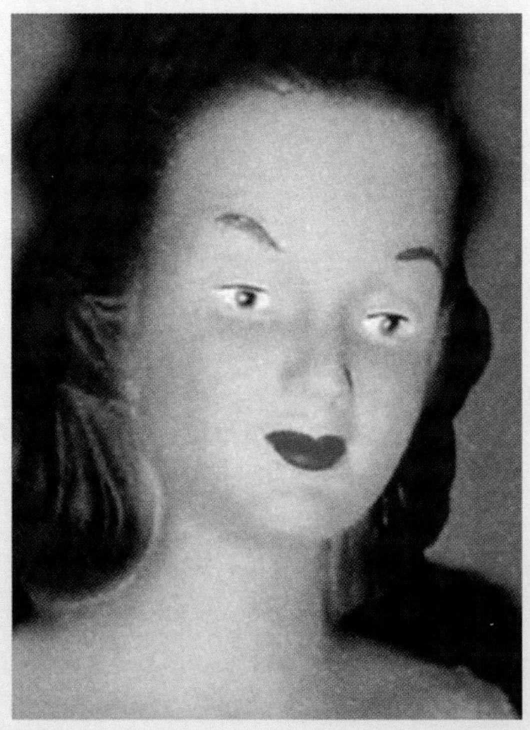

adult patterns. This was intended to show women how the adult version would look when completed. These mini mannequins measured 30-1/4in (77cm) with removable arms to assist in dressing them. Margit Nilsen also made miniature children mannequins to show what children's patterns would look like when done in full scale. These are the most difficult to find today. These mannequins were called counter displays because they stood on a wooden base that held a place card telling the consumer the pattern number, how much material was needed, and what it would cost to make that particular outfit. The earlier mannequins were made of a composition base. They had molded, painted hair and shoes, and most came with painted eyes that looked as if they were closed. There were twelve different mannequins with different colored hair and with arms positioned so as to facilitate posing them in their many and varied outfits. The fashions for these mannequins ranged from bridal wear, to daywear, to evening wear. The later ones were made of hard vinyl and had almond shaped painted eyes and synthetic wigs. These Margit Nilsen display dolls are very hard to come by today since some were destroyed and most of the remaining examples are in private collections.

Other companies such as Butterick, Simplicity, and Singer jumped on the bandwagon as well and produced their own miniature display mannequins. These miniature mannequins were also used for displaying regular size fashions, sewn from a pattern, in miniature. The different pattern companies produced and distributed most of these mannequins as a way of promoting their patterns without using a large quantity of fabric. Using very little fabric and display space, the mannequins could be placed on a counter top or used as a small window display. Space and fabric was at a premium especially during the war years. The United States government limited the amount of fabric that could be used in the manufacturing of

Top to Bottom:
Flexees lingerie display mannequin. Notice the name on the chest.

This is the same Flexees display mannequin. This close-up shows the style of her hair.

This close-up shows the face of a Nilsen display mannequin.

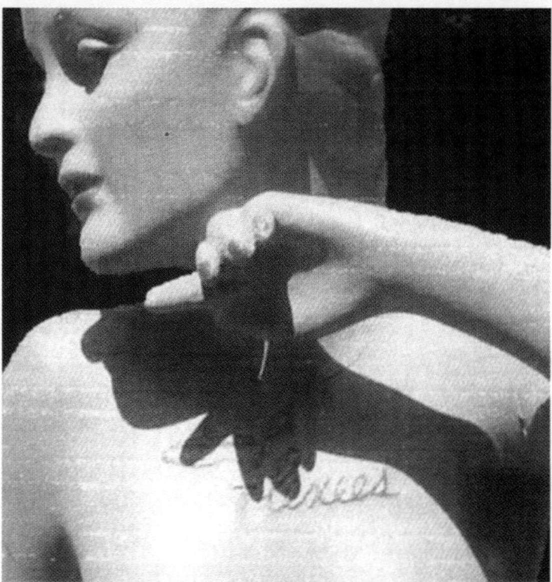

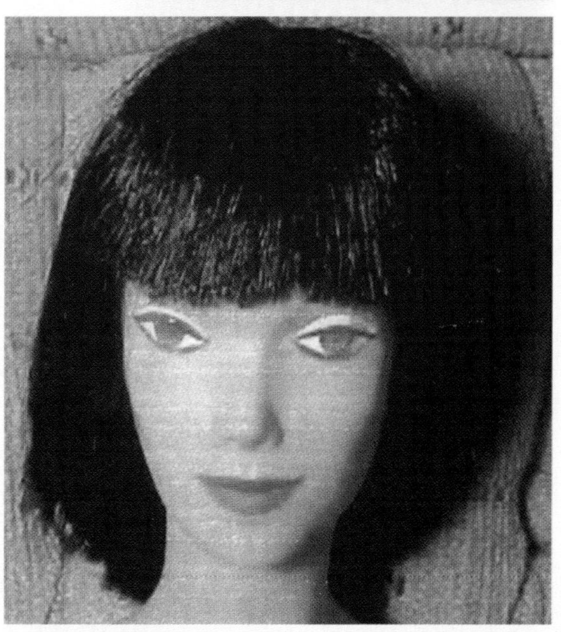

clothing and accessories. Some manufactures and retail stores that used more than the allotted amount of fabric were given citations and fines. Realizing the need to conserve fabric and the need for space, these mannequins were made smaller than the regular mannequins were. They ranged in size from 12-1/2in (32cm) up to 36in (91cm) and were made of wood, composition, rubber, or vinyl. Usually the pattern was put in a display and set next to the mini mannequin. Like McCall's mannequins, they gave the customer the opportunity of seeing what outfits would look like after it was completed without the expense of yards of fabric. Fashions for these mini mannequins ranged from simple daywear to elaborate gowns. Most outfits were changed every few weeks to keep customers interested in new patterns, but some elaborate costumes were permanently stapled to the mannequin's body. They also made miniature head mannequins to display hats, scarves, and jewelry. Mini mannequins were also very popular in displaying bridal wear since fine fabrics such as silk and nylon were being requisitioned for the war effort and being used in ammunition bags and parachutes. By using a 14in (36cm) display mannequin, a store owner or pattern company could considerably decrease the amount of fabric needed to make a replica of the gown.

I have some mannequins whose arms are removable to make dressing them easier. I also have some with a solid body where the outfit was just molded to the body of the mannequin. Of those mannequins that had removable arms, some had pull-off arms with posts while others had square metal pegs that slid into the shoulder. Still others had metal armatures to hook them into place at the shoulder like the lifelike store mannequins of the time. Most of the time the lower torso was one solid molded piece and only the arms

Close-up of a 19in (49cm) Simplicity display mannequin of the 1940's.

were removable. These mannequins are now great examples of fashion from the 1930's through the 1960's and are highly sought after.

Some miniature mannequins were used in other types of advertising for stores. They were used to advertise everything from Ace Bandages to Clinic shoes to Duofold (men's long underwear). The best way to find these dolls today is by scouring the antique shops, garage sales, rummage sales, and the Internet. Expect to pay a hefty price for some of these mannequins, especially if they are a Margit Nilsen or a Hindsgaul. Remember that Butterick, Simplicity, and McCall all had their own mannequins not to mention the off brand mannequin dolls and the advertising mannequins, so there are quite a few out there.

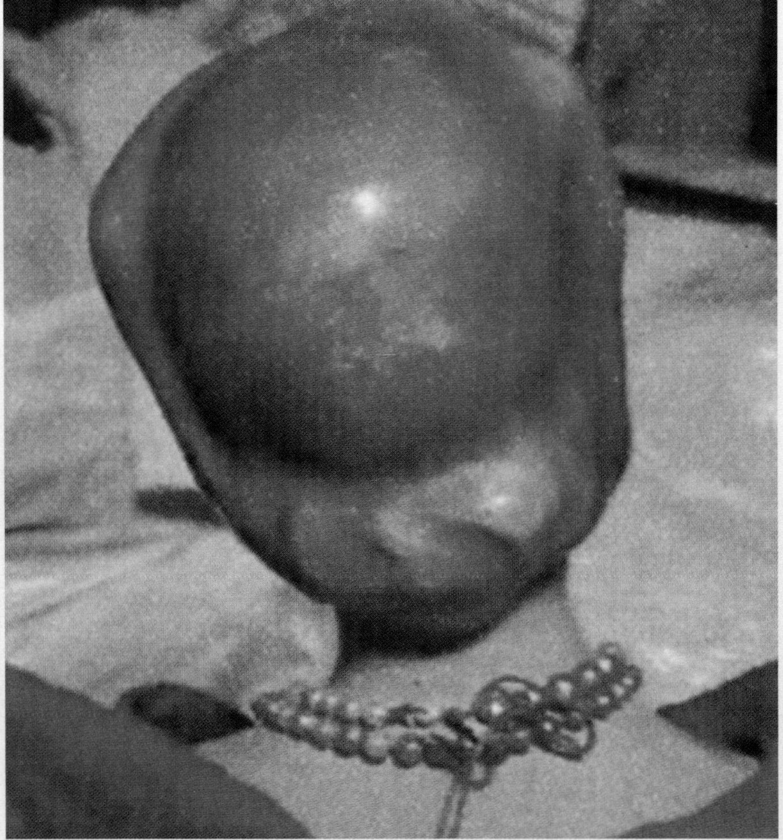

This back view is of a 1940's Simplicity display mannequin's head.

This is a 6in (15cm) half-mannequin store display from the 1940's.

Top to Bottom:
This close-up shows that she is missing her thumbs.

Here you can see the mannequin's partial body.

This is a 14in (36cm) display bride from the 1940's. A store employee made the outfit.

Left: The back view of the gown.

Below: These two 1940's display mannequins have the same body mold but have different hair paint and face paint.

1940's display bride mannequin wearing a hand-made wedding gown.

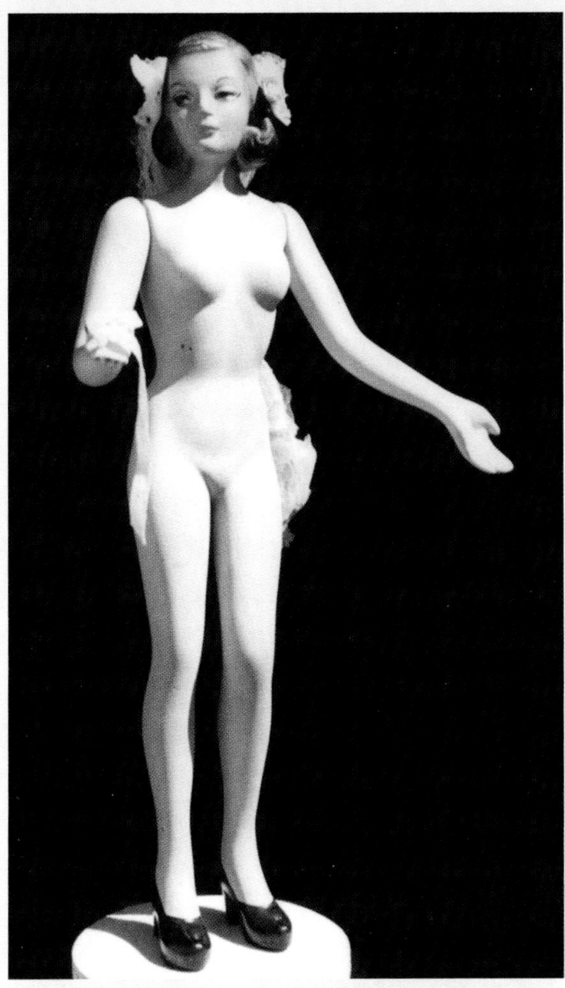

Left: This bridal miniature mannequin has removable arms and painted on formed high heel shoes.

Below Left: The back view of the bridal mannequin shows holes in her back where the dress was stapled to her.

Below: This front view of the bridal miniature display mannequin shows the exceptional sculpting that is very true to form.

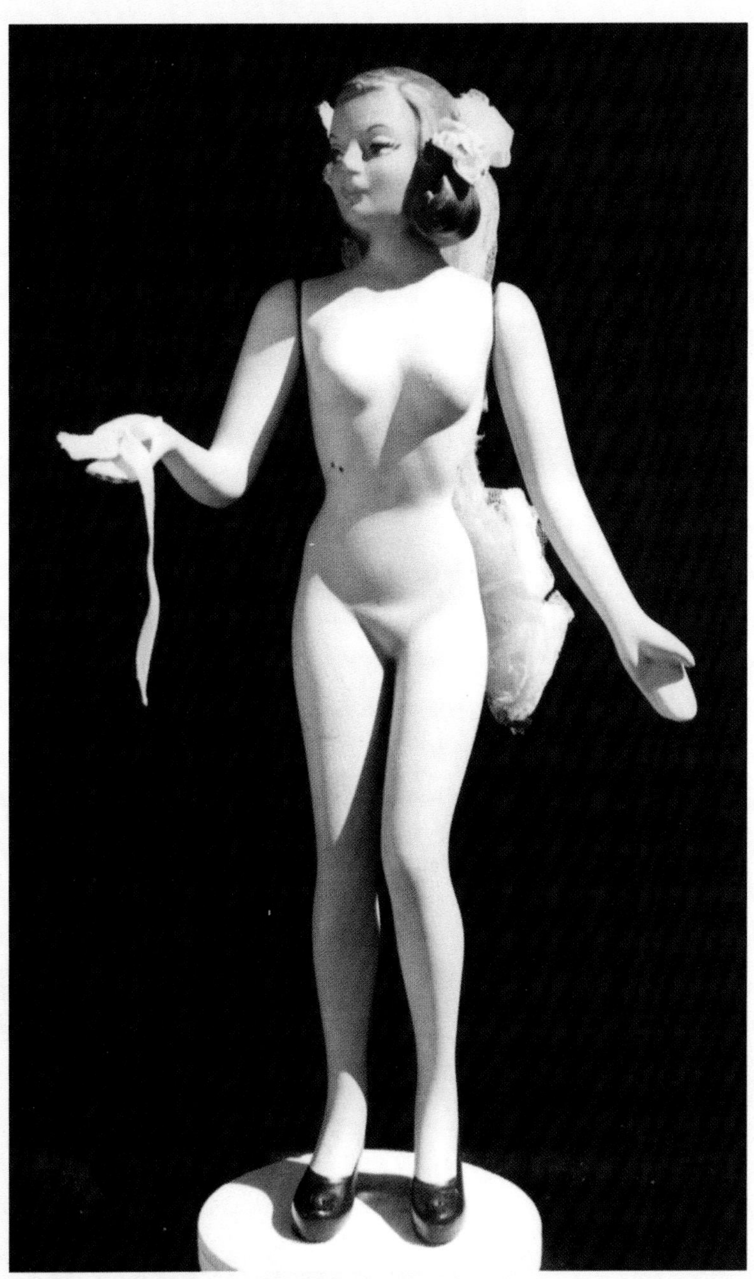

15in (38cm) vintage miniature bridal display mannequin from the 1950's. She is not a full mannequin as she has a cone under the skirt instead of legs.

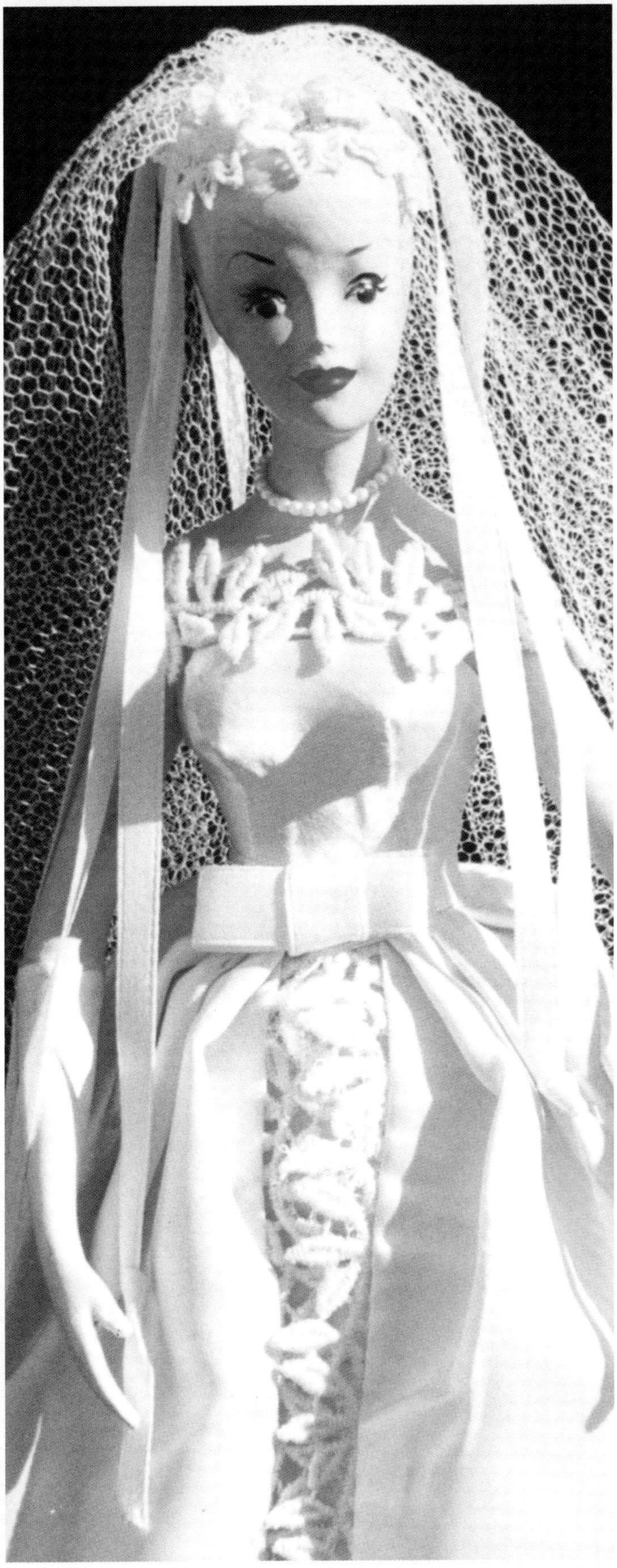

Left: Close-up of the vintage bridal display mannequin.

Below: This photo shows the cone used for her body rather than legs.

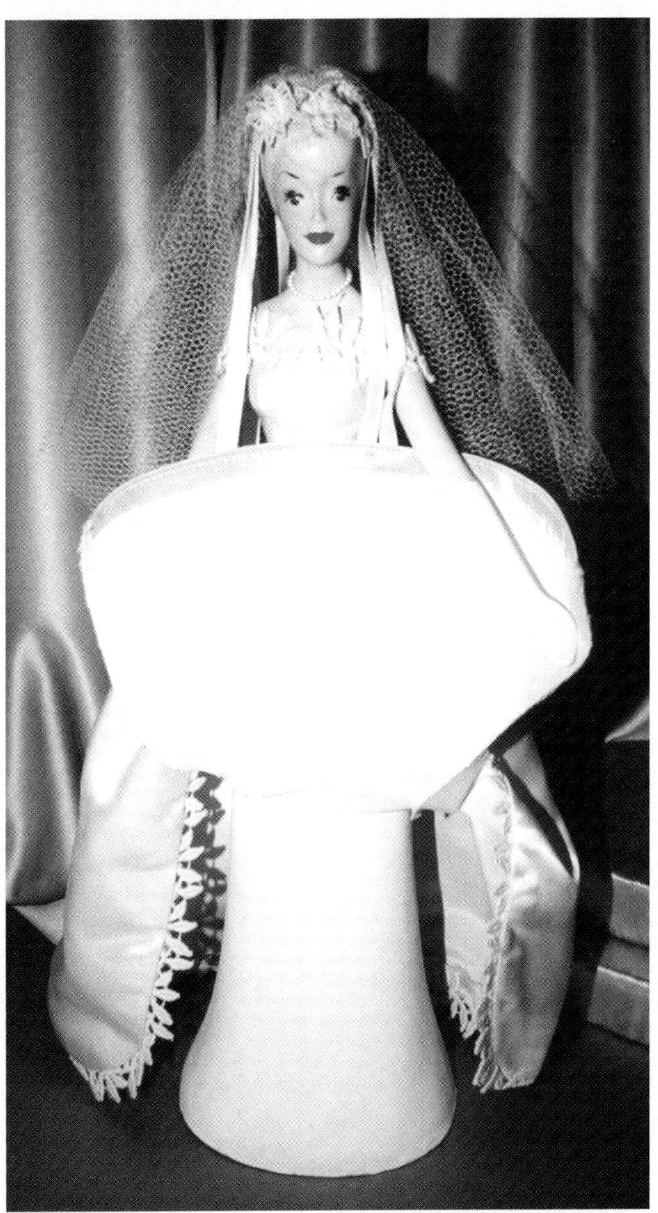

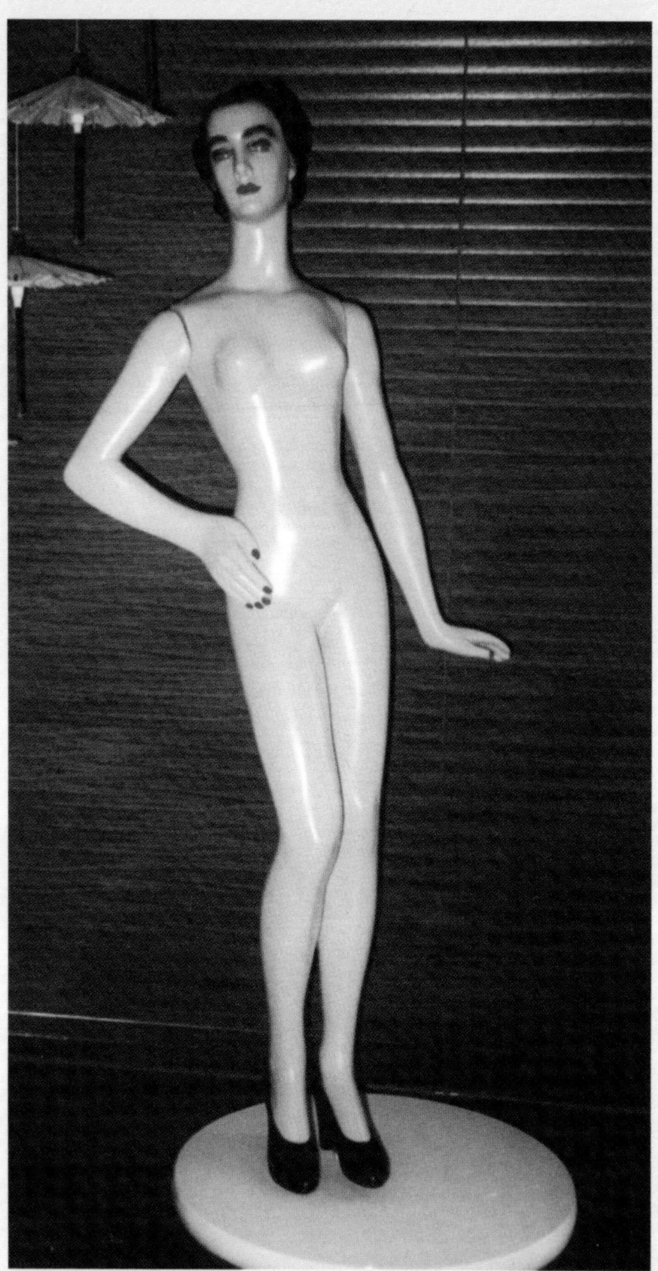

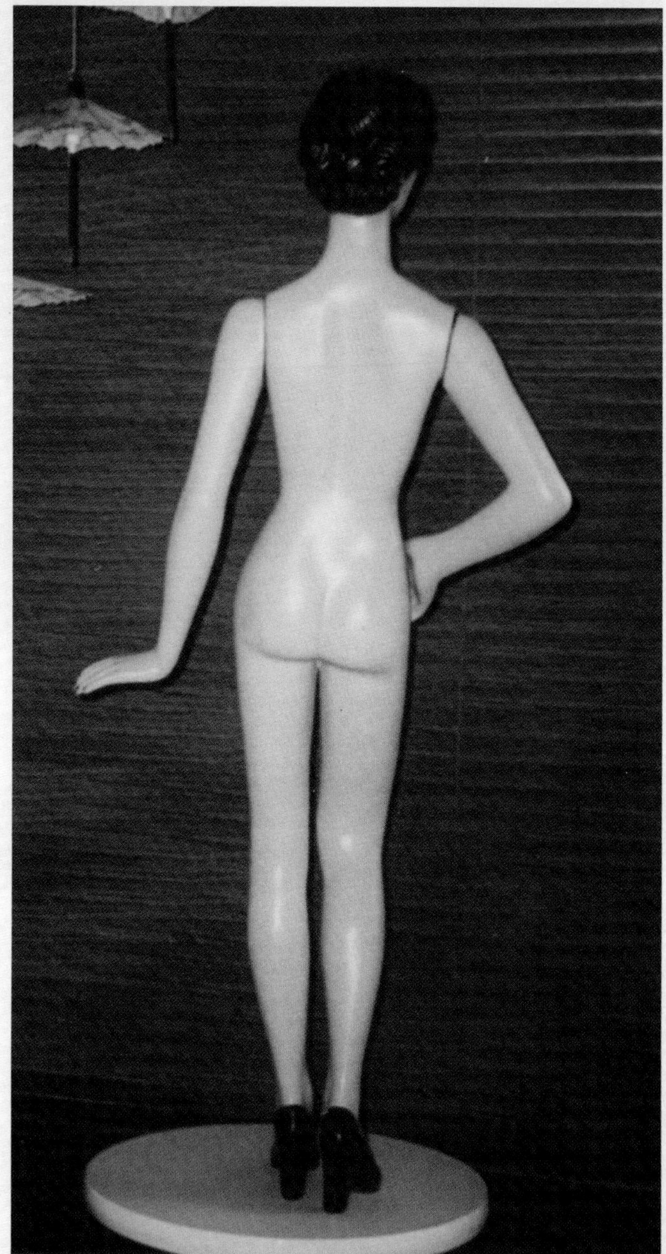

1940's display mannequin with removable arms for easy dressing. She is 31in (79cm) tall and is from the collection of Connie and Brent George.

This photo shows the back view of the display mannequin.

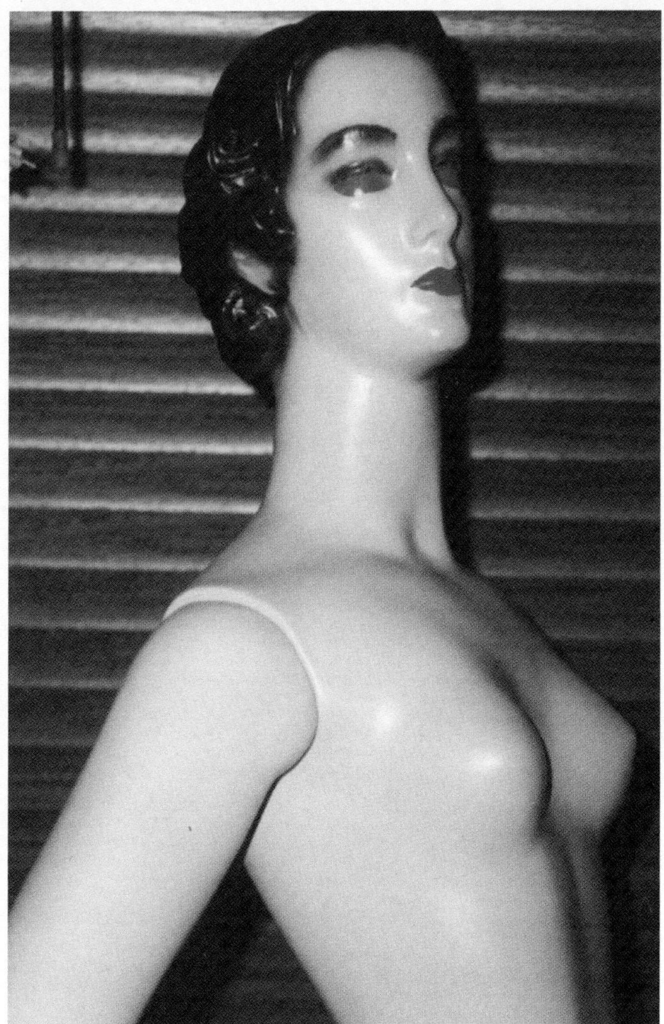

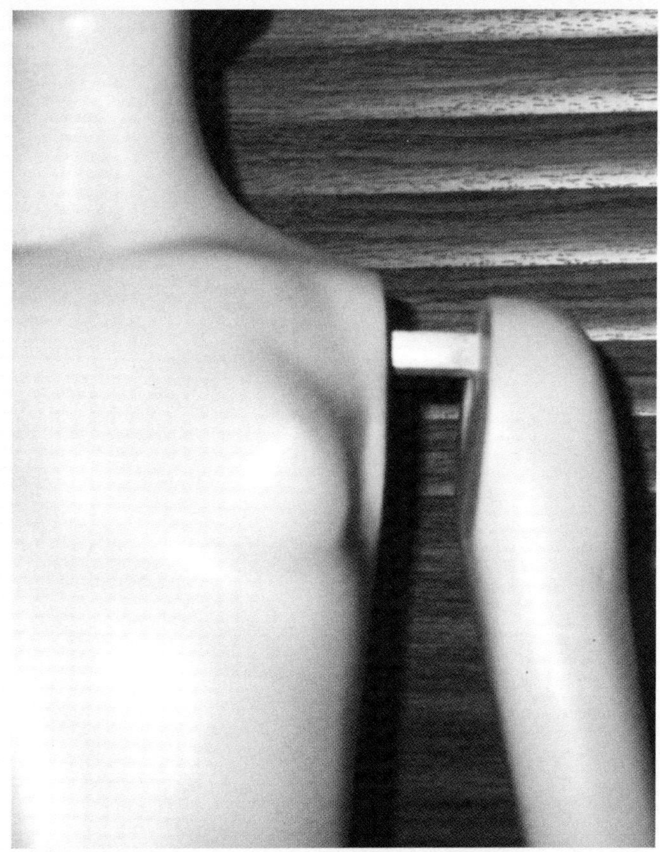

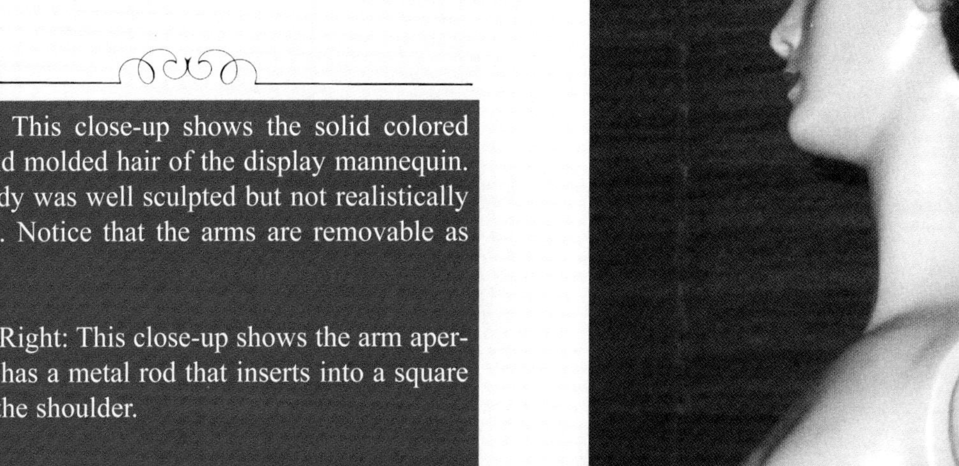

Above: This close-up shows the solid colored eyes and molded hair of the display mannequin. The body was well sculpted but not realistically painted. Notice that the arms are removable as well.

Above Right: This close-up shows the arm aperture. It has a metal rod that inserts into a square slot in the shoulder.

Right: Here is a view of the square slot in which the metal rod in the arm is inserted.

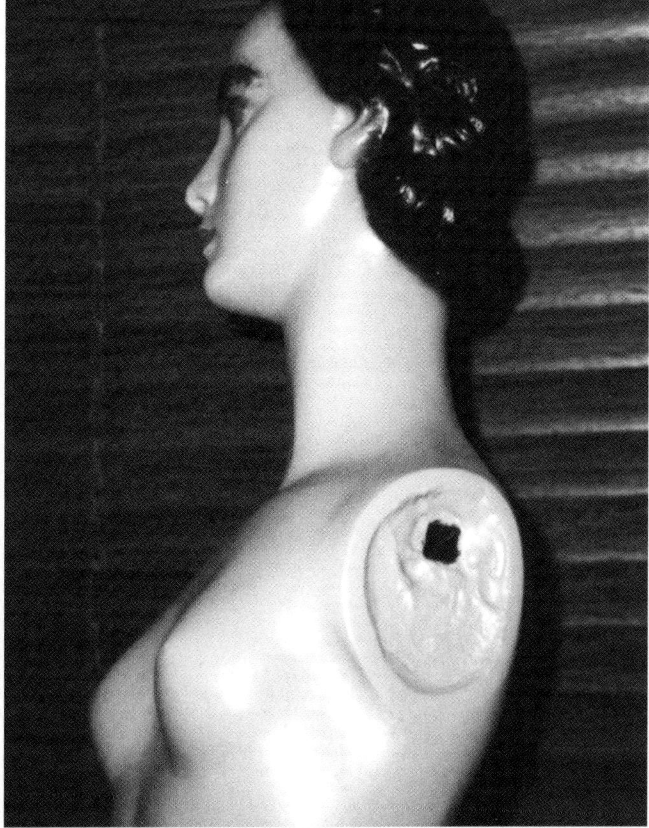

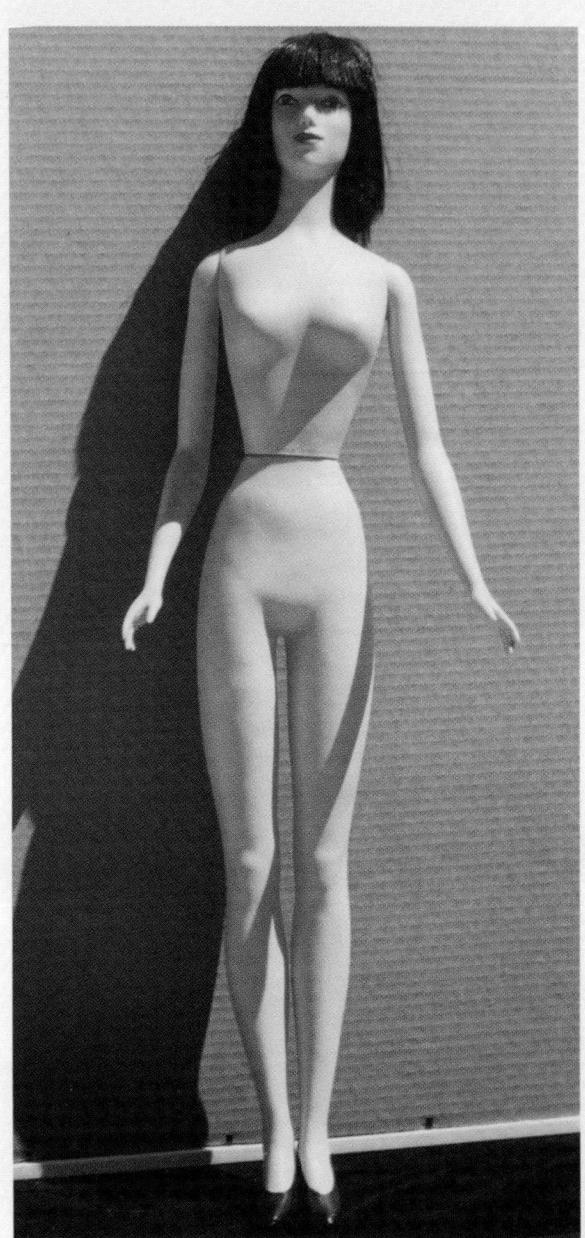

Margit Nilsen 21in (53cm) display mannequin from the 1960's.

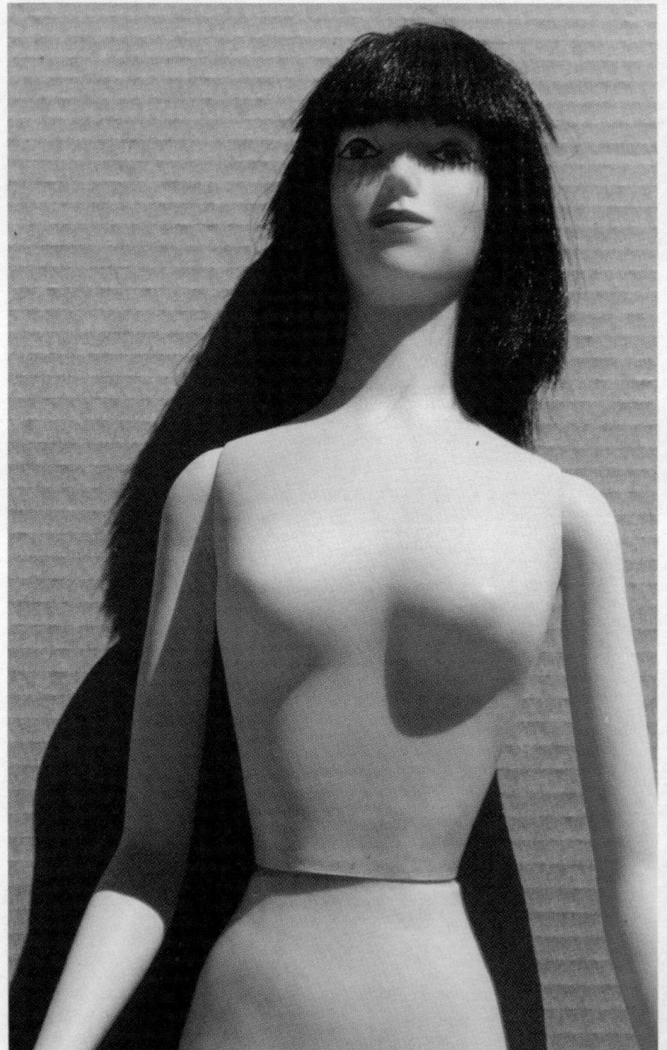

Close-up of the Margit Nilsen mannequin.

This is a hand-carved fully jointed miniature mannequin.

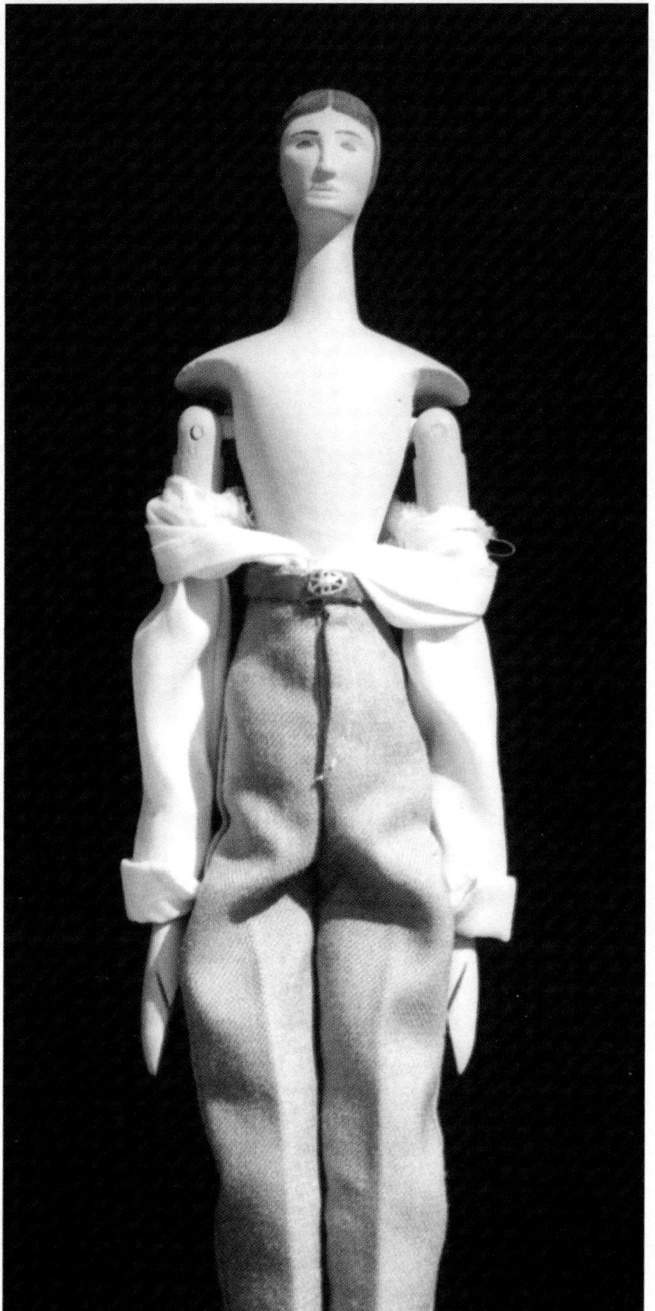

Here you can see the joints in this mannequin's shoulders.

Above: Hand-made stuffed mannequin with a mohair wig. She is from the 1950's.

Above Right: This 9in (23cm) Shackman mannequin doll is from the 1960's. She has a wooden body with a bisque head.

Right: This is an *ACE Bandage* display mannequin.

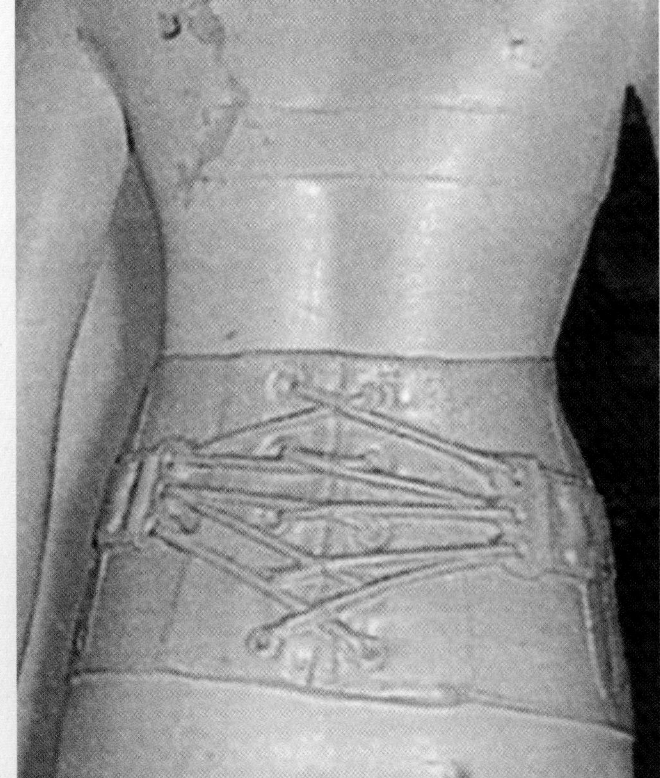

Mannequin Sewing Dolls

Miniature mannequins were used as teaching tools for children. They were both educational and fun to play with. Women were typically expected to know how to sew for their families and to teach their daughters how to sew. Due to low incomes during the depression and cloth shortages during the World Wars, pattern companies, such as Butterick, Simplicity, McCalls and Singer, created these dolls to teach sewing skills to young girls or people just learning how to sew while conserving fabric. Other companies that made versions of these sewing mannequins were Transogram and Stitchcraft.

Companies sold these mannequins in sewing kits that typically included patterns, instruction booklets, material, scissors, thread, measuring tapes, needles, and thimbles—everything one needed to begin sewing. The Singer Sewing Machine Company even included a miniature Singer sewing machine with some of their kits. The McCall sets included a little booklet entitled "Tricks in Sewing," which was very useful and covered topics such as how to take measurements, selecting fabrics, alteration hints, laying out your pattern, and fitting the patterns to the dolls. Some kits also had order forms for ordering more pattern sets. These mannequins usually required less than 1/4 yd (.23m) of material to make a garment. After making the garment in miniature, novice sewers could then buy a pattern in a larger size to make for themselves. The pattern numbers on the miniature patterns corresponded to the larger patterns.

The earlier dolls were made of a composition material. They were painted a flesh tone and had molded, painted hair and shoes. They had removable arms to make dressing them easier and prongs on the bottom of their feet in order to place them on a stand. Some of the early mannequins were also made of rubber with wooden dowels in the legs to enable them to be posed on their special stands.

These mannequins came in 12-1/2in (32cm) to 15in (38cm) sizes and had corresponding pattern sizes made for them. Some had names such as Suzanne, Peggy, and Marianne and came in a variety of sizes and hair colors. You can usually find these dolls in antiques shops or garage sales or even on the Internet. You can end up paying some pretty steep prices for these sewing mannequins especially the ones mint-in-the-box with all the accessories. You can still find plenty that are out of their boxes that may only have a pattern or two with them. The prices for these sewing dolls would be a lot easier on the budget. You might also think about just buying the pieces and putting the kits together over a period of time, as I have done with a lot of my sets. The next few chapters will look at the different miniature mannequin sewing kits that were produced by the pattern companies for children as well as some off-brand children's sewing kits.

Singer mannequin on the left and Peggy the mannequin on the right.

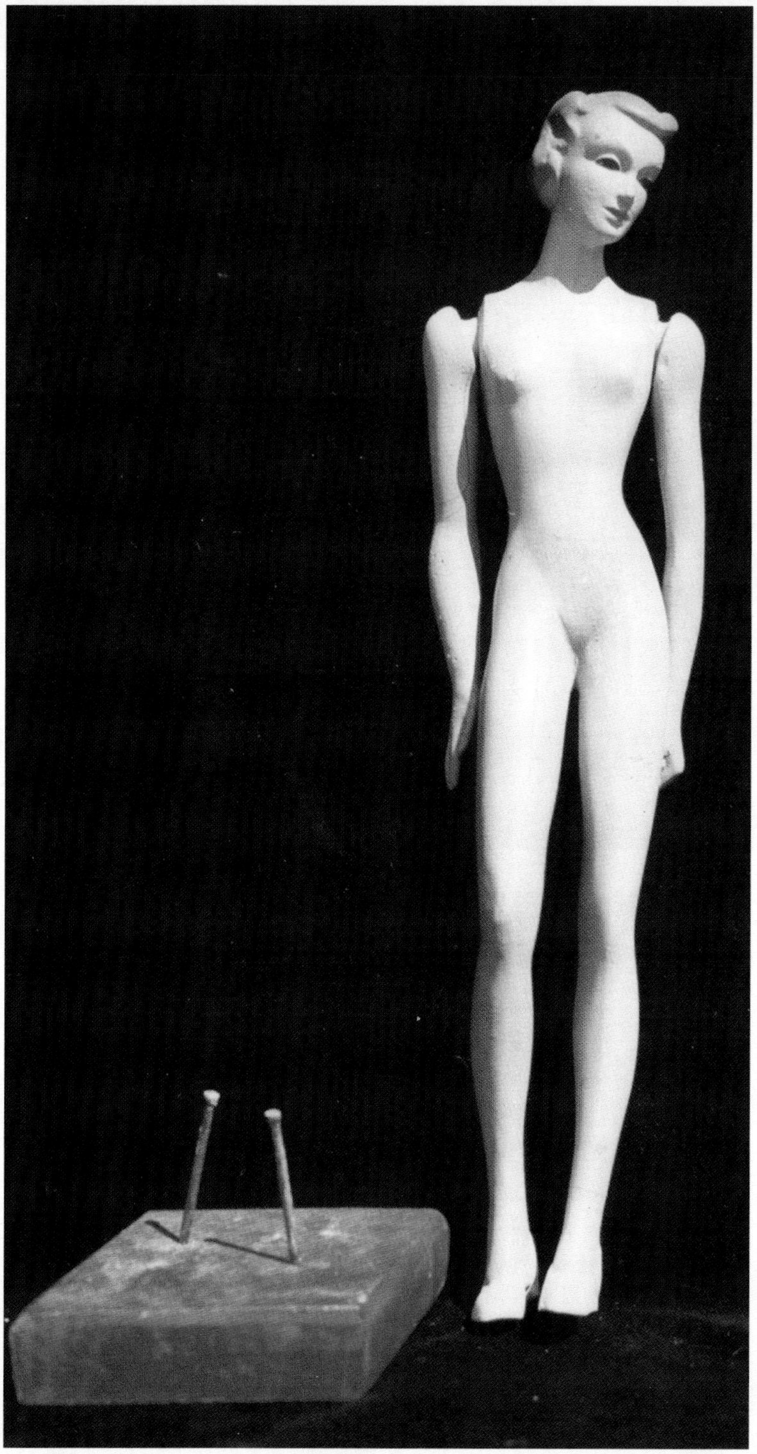

A 12in (31cm) Susanne mannequin doll. She was one of the first made. Here you can see her stand which says, "From a mother to her daughter on Dec 25th 1941."

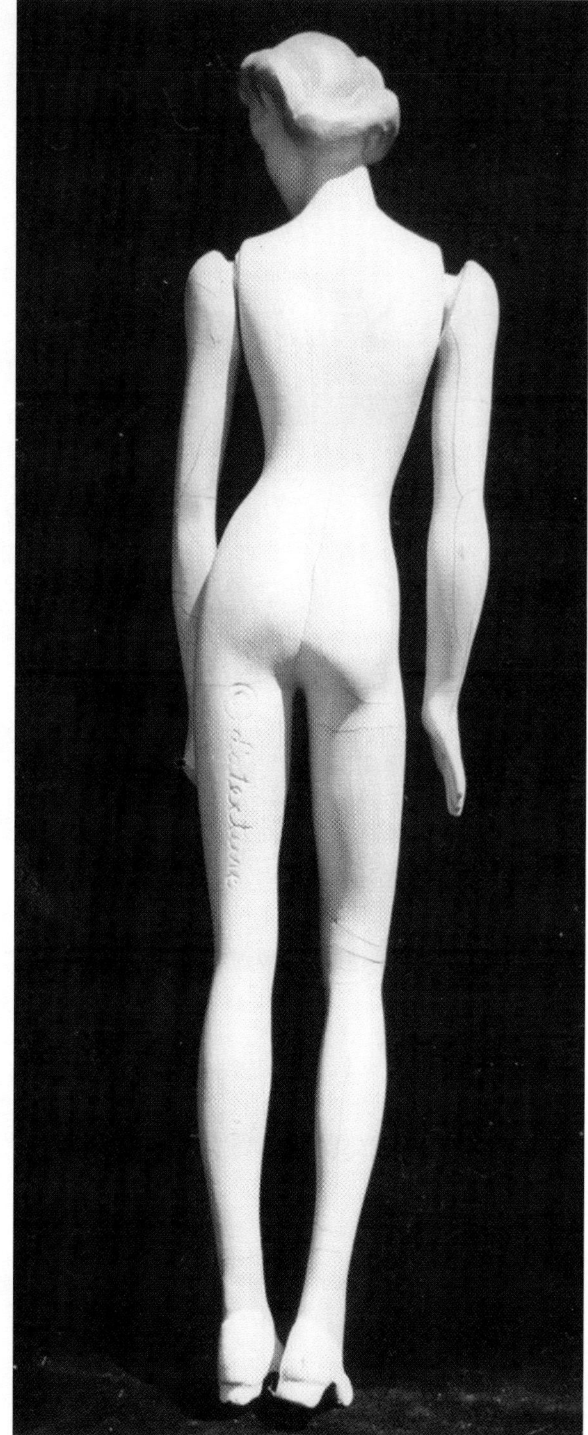

Latexture is stamped on the leg of this Susanne mannequin doll from 1941.

Three patterns came with the Susanne Sewing Kit: Day Dress #2001, Nurse's Uniform #2002, and Nurse's Cape #2004.

Susanne's Fashion Show

Susanne is not just an ordinary doll. She is a true miniature manikin of a young girl, made of flexible, durable material that is used for full sized fashion figures.

Like all good manikins, Susanne has detachable arms to make it easy to dress and undress her. To remove the arms just pull them out gently at the shoulder.

In order to make the figure stand erect, place it on the base with the two pins in the holes of the feet.

Now she is ready to try on her new clothes. You will find the pat[illegible]s for making her clothes.

You can use the patterns over and over if you handle them carefully, and develop lots of ideas of your own.

You will find it is not at all difficult to learn how dresses are made. We wish you lots of fun and success.

Judith.

This page came with the Susanne mannequin doll. It was titled "Susanne's Fashion Show."

Butterick Sewing Kits

In 1949, Educational Crafts Co. in New York City made the Junior Miss Fashion Designing Set with Mannequin for the Butterick Pattern Company. The kit included a 13in (33cm) composition mannequin with stand, six Butterick patterns, and material for making dresses. One of the pattern sets included a bridal gown, one-piece dirndl frock, and party frock. A second set included patterns for a wave uniform, wac uniform, and nurses uniform in addition to a "Sewright" booklet. The back of these patterns stated that the consumer could learn how to sew using approximately 1/4 yd (.23m) of fabric. Because these patterns were usually glued into the top of the box, use caution if you want to remove them. The company also made an earlier version in the 1930's. That doll was smaller than the later ones and had a different hair and face mold. The pattern that came with her was in black and white rather than color and came with the one-piece dirndl gown, party frock, and a nurses uniform instead of the bridal gown.

Ideal Toy Corp. in New York City made the Butterick Sew-Easy Designing Set, which looked like a small suitcase. It came with a rubber 12-1/2in (32cm) mannequin that had dowels inside her legs that fit inside her round metal stand. She also came with two pattern packages that consisted of three patterns each from the Butterick Pattern Company. These were miniature versions of the adult patterns. The set also included thread, thimble, measuring tape, and needle threader.

Another similar version of the kit was made by the Singer Manufacturing Company, and included the same 12-1/2in (32cm) rubber mannequin with different Butterick patterns, tape measure, needle threader, thimble, and sewing handbook. It also came in the same suitcase kit.

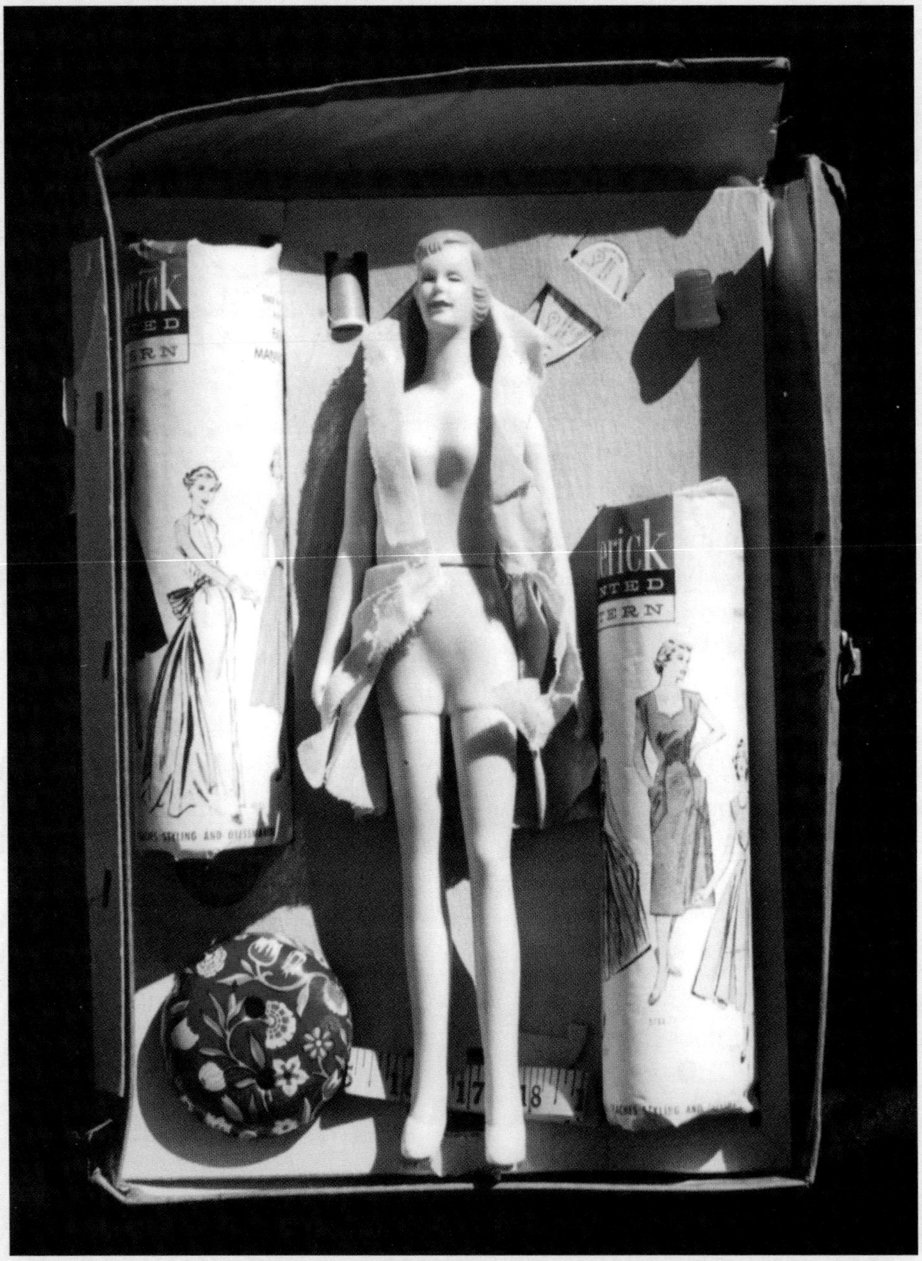

Ideal Butterick Sew-Easy Designing Set made by Ideal Toy Corporation, New York 1949. This set included a lifelike mannequin, six Butterick patterns that fit the mannequin, sewing accessories and complete instructions.

Here is the inside cover of the Ideal Butterick Sew-Easy Designing Set from 1949.

Here is the front cover of the Ideal Butterick Sew-Easy Designing Set that "teaches you to sew." It is very similar to the Singer mannequin kit.

These Butterick patterns were made for the Ideal Butterick Sew-Easy Designing Set. Patterns also came in adult sizes (left to right): #5979, #6083, #5917, #6057, #5744, and #6015.

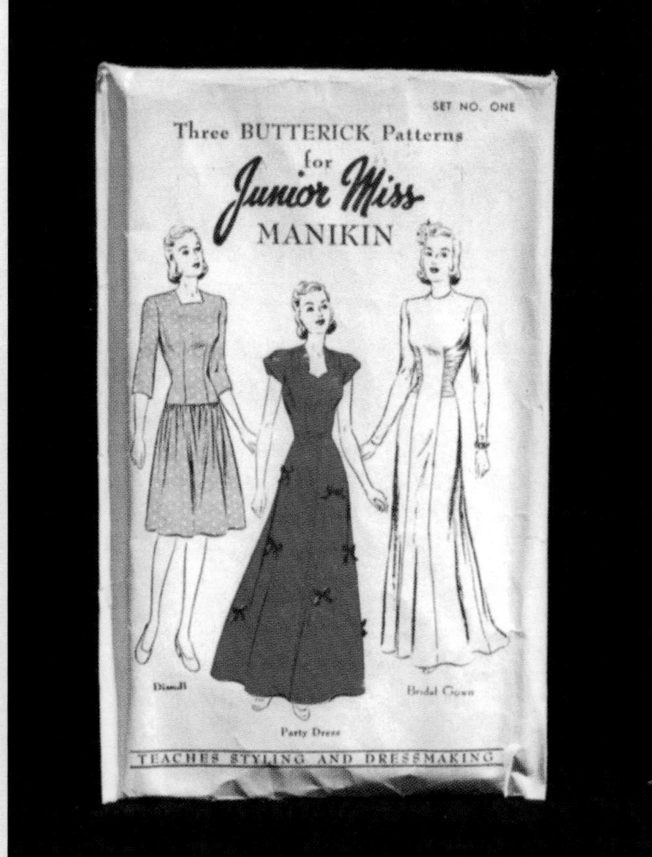

Butterick Pattern Set No. One that came with the Junior Miss Fashion Designing Set.

Junior Miss Mannequin Designing Set No. 10 included a 13in (33cm) doll with stand, and Butterick Pattern Set No. One. The fabric and "Sewright" booklet were manufactured by Educational Crafts Co. around 1949.

The sewing mannequin on the left is an earlier version of the Butterick Junior Miss Fashion Designing Set.

McCall Sewing Kits

In 1942, the Dritz-Traum Company Incorporated, in New York City made Peggy The Modern Fashion Model for the McCall Pattern Company. This kit was intended to help young girls learn how to sew as well as conserve fabrics. I could find no markings on the McCall sewing kits that I have, though there might be some that have marks. One of the kits included a 15in (38cm) mannequin doll and came in a red, white, and blue striped double box that opened in the middle. This set consisted of a display half mannequin, 4in (10cm) talon zipper, sewing needles, thimble, thread, material, "Tricks in Sewing" booklet, and a small packet of nails that the sewer had to hammer into a wooden stand to put through the holes in the mannequin's feet. It also included three patterns—6600-1 a Nurses Uniform, 6600-2 a Princess Dress, and 6600-3 a Daytime or Date Dress. These patterns measured about 4in x 3in (10cm x 8cm) in diameter. This kit also had a little pamphlet that told you how to remove the doll's arms in order to keep from breaking them (which was very easy to do). They also made a smaller version of Peggy, which came in a shoebox-shaped box with red, white, and blue stripes on the back of the box. This came with a 12in (31cm) mannequin doll, a "Tricks in Sewing" booklet, and only one pattern—6600-2 the Princess Dress. The booklet gave very helpful hints for sewing clothing for the mannequin doll.

McCall Peggy Mannequin Sewing Kit included a mannequin doll, half mannequin, sewing accessories, "Tricks in Sewing" booklet, and McCall Patterns.

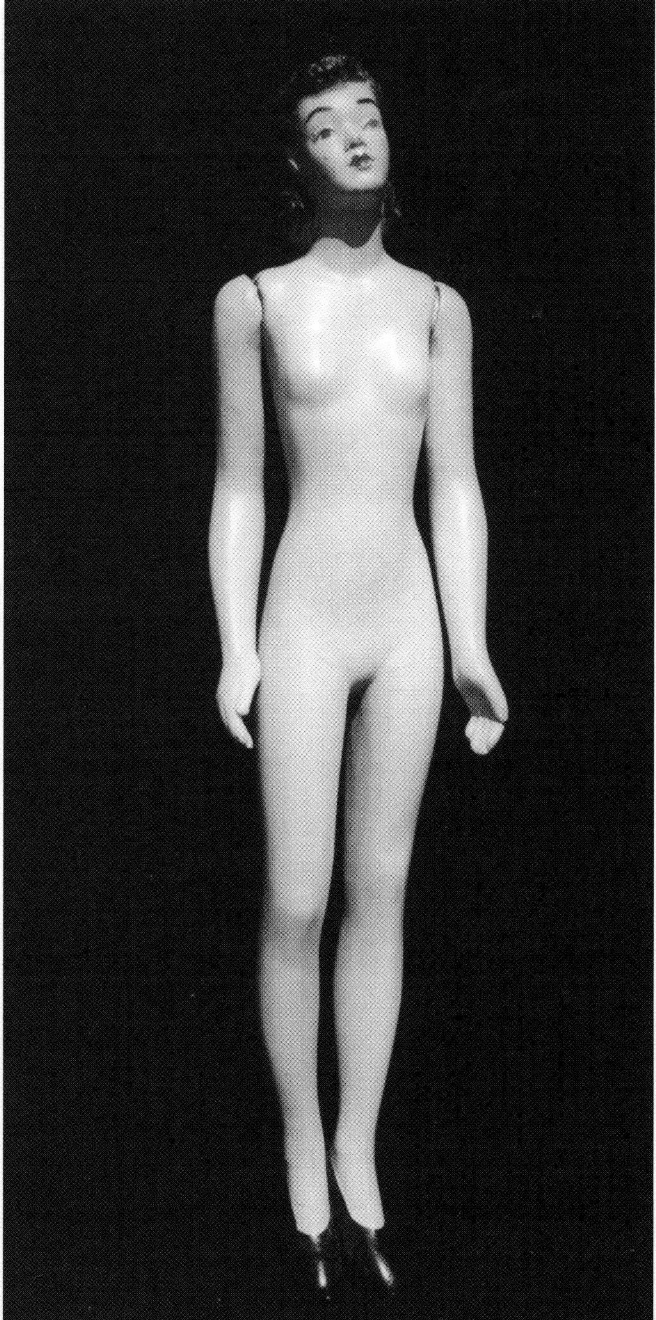

McCall patterns that were included with Peggy came in adult sizes #6600-2, #6600-3, and #6600-1.

Peggy the Modern Fashion Model with brunette hair. She is harder to find than the blonde version.

McCall's Peggy the Modern Fashion Model Sewing Kit included a 12-1/2in (32cm) mannequin and McCall pattern #6600-1 manufactured by Dritz-Traum Co. in 1942.

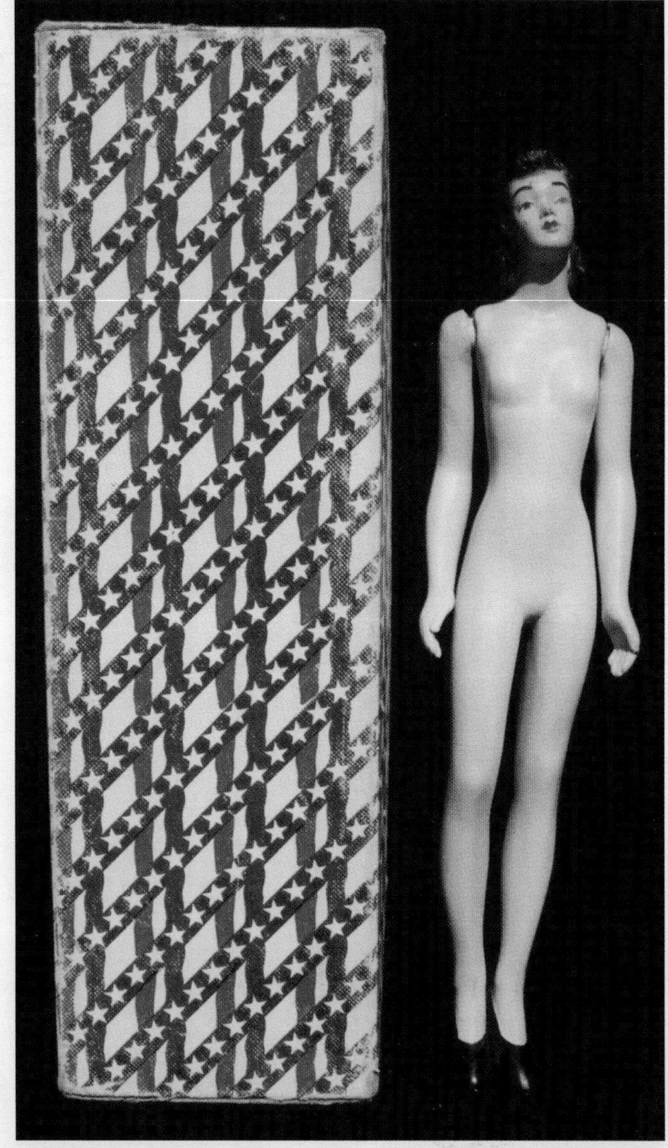

Here is Peggy with the back of her box.

Simplicity Sewing Kits

Latexture Products Inc. in New York City made the Fashiondol kits for the Simplicity Pattern Company in the 1940's. They created a mannequin that was supposed to resemble a miniature teenage girl. It was made of a plastic material, but was not flexible. Because the War Production Program required rubber, which had been used in the manufacture of these mannequins, the company had to change materials in order to continue making them. Extra patterns could be ordered for these dolls by sending in 25¢ for a set of three patterns. There were eight sets of patterns for the 12-1/2in (32cm) mannequin and eight for the 15in (38cm) mannequin. The pattern sets included such outfits as pinafores, slips and panties, housecoats, bathing suits, afternoon dresses, Army uniforms, and dinner dresses. These kits also included a sewing book that gave tips on the "How's and Why's of Good Dressmaking". You could find tips for topics such as pattern alterations to suit your figure, pointers on cutting, transferring the markings of patterns to garment pieces, a needle and thread guide, getting the most out of your sewing machine, the right way to pin and baste. Latexture Products Inc. produced Suzanne the Mannequin Doll as well as the Marianne Fashion Designing Set. In one set, you got the 15in (38cm) Suzanne doll with stand and three patterns in addition to a half mannequin for displaying your finished work. Fabric, thread, thimble, tape measure, and ordering form for ordering more patterns were also part of the set. Another 15in (38cm) Suzanne doll came in a mailing box with a place for address information. A pattern was also included with this version. The 12-1/2in (32cm) Marianne doll came in her own special box including three patterns, fabric for her first dress, tape measure, sewing booklet, and thread. The extra patterns could be ordered for 25¢.

A 15in (38cm) Suzanne the Mannequin Doll with a dress made from one of the miniature mannequin patterns. She is from the collection of Debbie Weinstein.

Above: Simplicity Miniature Fashions Set came with a 12-1/2in (32cm) mannequin, four patterns, a measuring tape, thread, stand, and sewing booklet.

Right: Here you can see the Simplicity Miniature Fashions box set #102 made by Latexture Products, Inc. 1949. The price was originally $2.00.

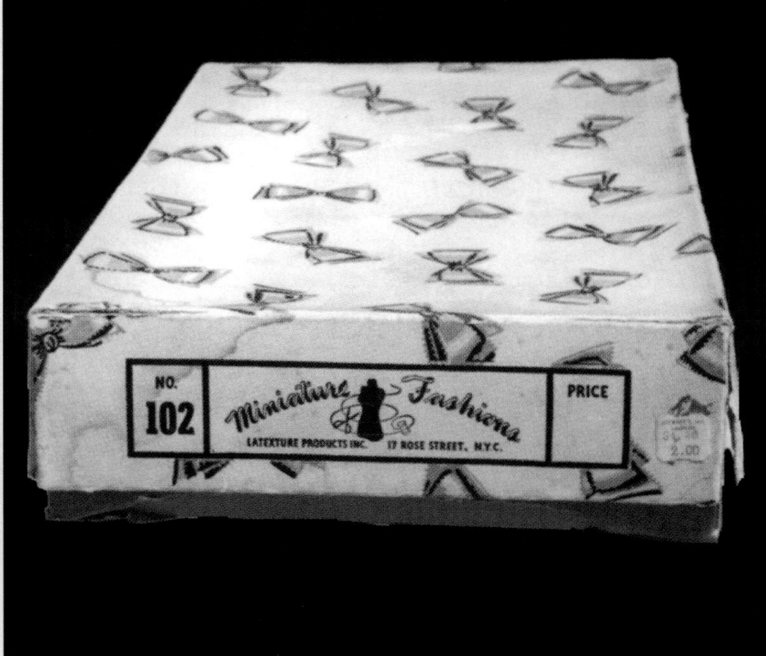

Here is another version of the Simplicity Miniature Fashions Set with pattern #4401, a wooden base, a sewing handbook, tape measure, and a piece of fabric. The Latexture Products, Co. manufactured this set in 1943.

These are Simplicity patterns included with the Miniature Fashions kit by Latexture Products, Inc. Pattern numbers left to right are: 4359, 4387, 4710, and 4401.

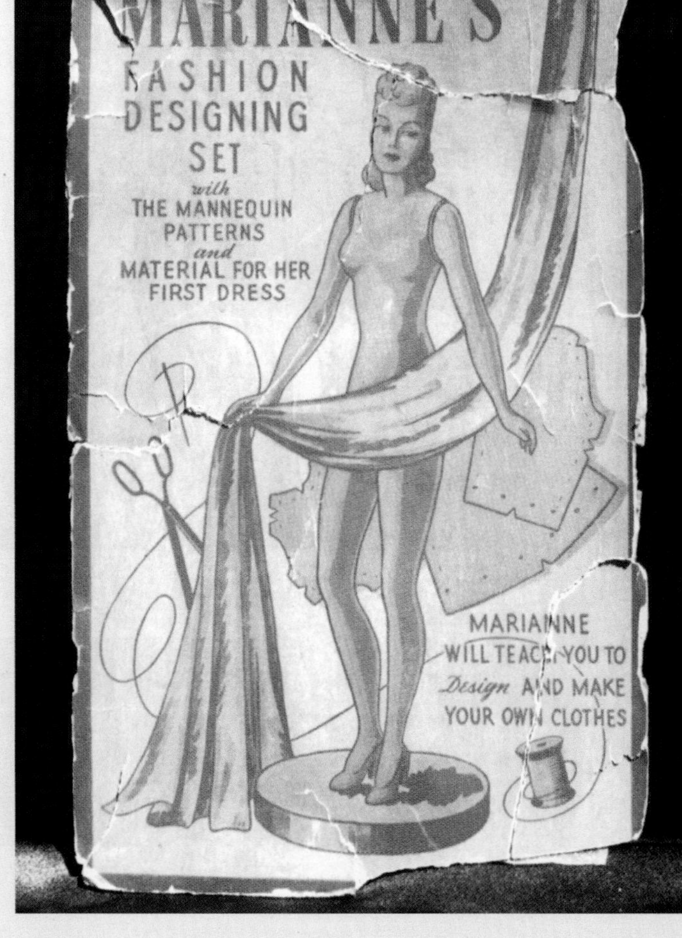

Marianne's Fashion Designing Set included a 12-1/2in (32cm) mannequin, patterns, material, and accessories.

Here is Marianne next to what is left of her box.

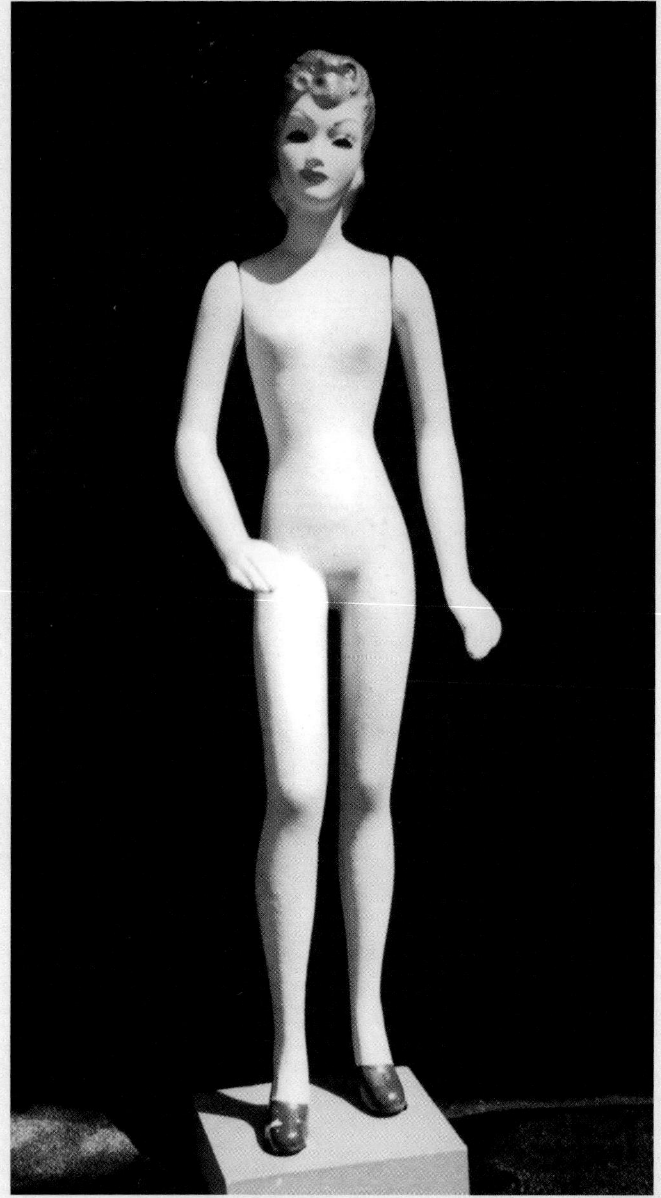

A 12-1/2in (32cm) Marianne Mannequin Doll with molded red hair.

Three patterns came with Marianne: #103, #102, and #101.

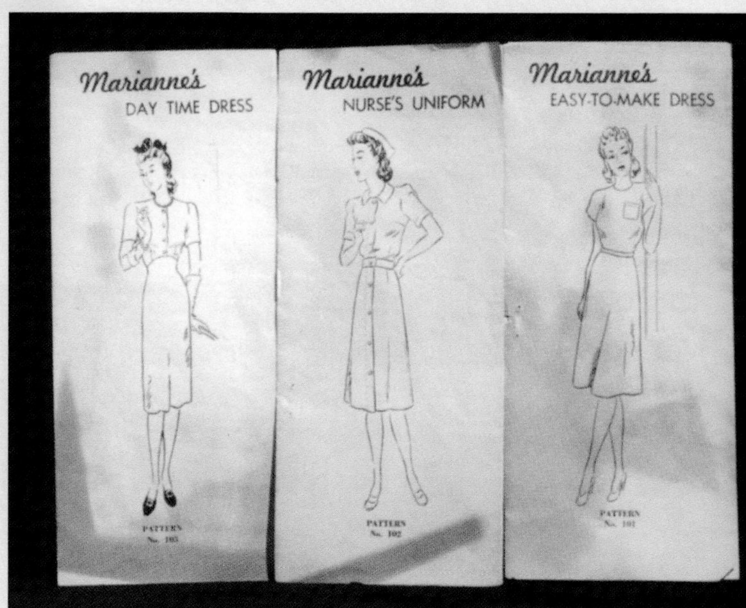

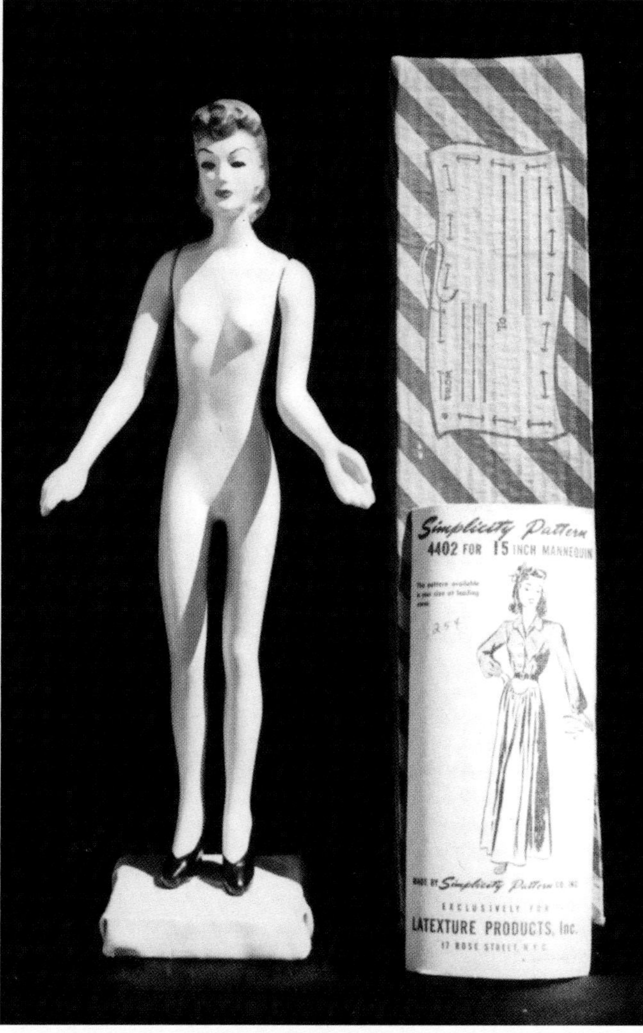

Here is a 15in (38cm) Suzanne mannequin with pattern #4402.

This 1940's Suzanne is shown in her shipping box.

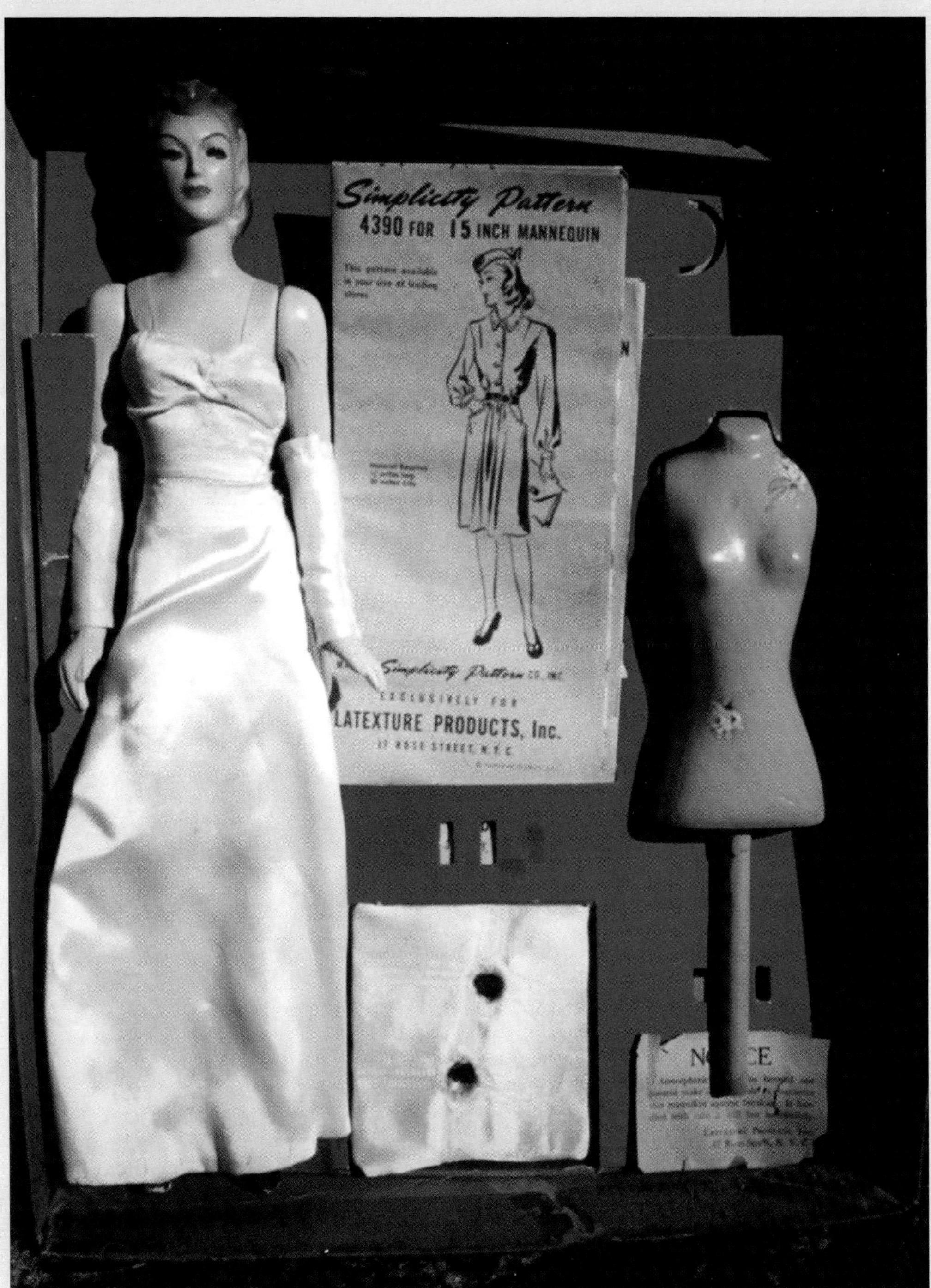

Suzanne the Mannequin by Latexture Products, Inc. The design kit included a 15in (38cm) mannequin, three Simplicity patterns, a dress form, and accessories.

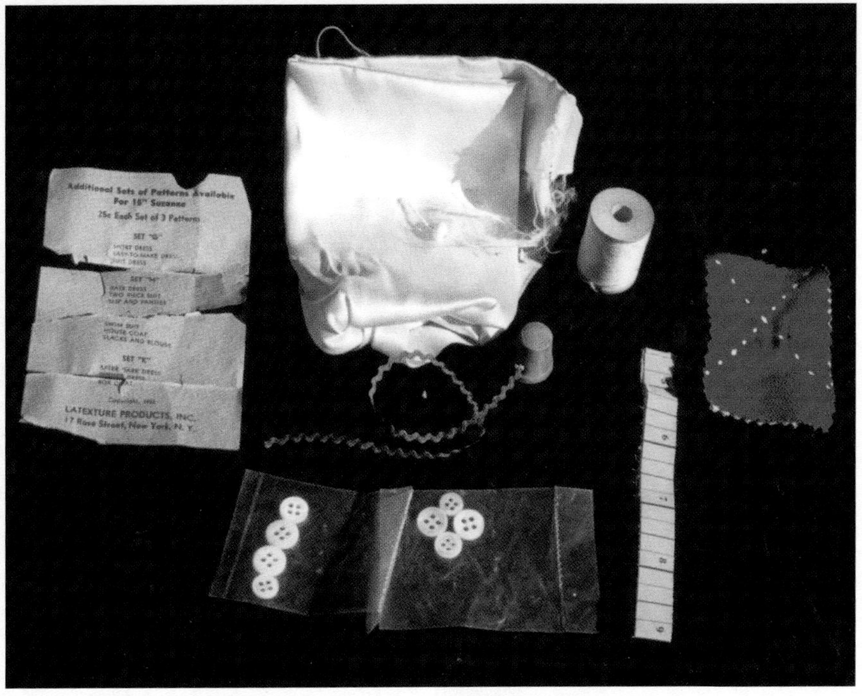

These accessories were included with the Suzanne mannequin kit. Notice that there are buttons, silk material, thread, a measuring tape, thimble, and instructions for ordering more patterns.

Above: This sewing booklet was included with the Miniature Fashions kit.

Right: These patterns fit the Suzanne the Mannequin doll. They also came in adult sizes. The numbers are #4394, #4402, and #4390 respectively.

Both of these dolls are from the Suzanne the Mannequin sewing kit. Notice the difference in their arms.

Singer Sewing Kits

W. Smith Industries made the Singer Mannequin Doll Set expressly for The Singer MFG. Co. These kits came in a cardboard suitcase with a metal latch for ease of traveling. It showed an illustration of a young girl on the front, dressing a mannequin doll. This kit included a 12in (31cm) rubber mannequin doll, six Butterick patterns, tape measure, thimble, needle threader, and a sewing handbook. The inside cover of the handbook featured a picture of a miniature Singer Sew-handy sewing machine from 1949. The caption under it read, "A Real Singer Sewing Machine, Sturdy, Completely safe, No bobbins to wind. Just the thing to teach machine sewing to your child while she makes beautiful dresses for her Singer Mannikin Doll." Some of these kits came in a wooden suitcase and included a miniature singer

Here are six Butterick patterns and the sewing handbook from the Singer Mannikin Doll Set. They came in adult sizes as well. From left to right: #5366, #5100, #5354, #5460 or 5453, #5428, and #5547 or 5453.

sewing machine along with everything else. The patterns that were included with these kits were actual miniature reproductions of "grown-up" designs taken from the Butterick Pattern Catalog and complete in every way to the adult pattern. These patterns may seem a bit complicated for today's child to comprehend since sewing is not a basic skill taught to today's girls, but in the 1940's girls were taught sewing skills at a very early age and were therefore able to understand these patterns. Girls were usually taught to sew as soon as they could handle the concept of cutting, sewing, and fitting. The sewing handbook included with this kit was a dictionary of the sewing terms found in the instruction sheet. The book was arranged alphabetically so that any sewing term or word could be found very quickly in the Table of Contents. It gave instructions on basting, bias, binding, darts, facings, gathering, grain lines in fabric, hemming, notching, pressing, and slipstitching. At the end of the introduction, it invited interested parties to get information about sewing classes from the sewing teacher at any Singer Sewing Center.

W. Smith Industries made the Singer Mannikin Doll Set from 1949 exclusively for The Singer MFG. CO. The set included a 12in (31cm) rubber mannequin, stand, six Butterick patterns, a sewing booklet, thread, and accessories.

Front cover of the Singer Mannikin Doll Set.

This is the inside cover of the box. Notice the old fashioned child's Singer sewing machine.

Off-Brand Sewing Kits

Many of the smaller companies got into the sewing kit business during and after World War II, since sewing was such a widespread activity back in the 40's and 50's. There were numerous sewing kits made between the 40's and 50's—the companies discussed below are just a few of those that jumped on the bandwagon.

The "Little Traveler's Sewing Kit", a suit case sewing kit produced by the Transogram Company, Inc. in New York City came in several variations. One kit consisted of a small 6-1/2in (17cm) mannequin doll with molded hair and shoes and painted features. It had assorted colored thread, scissors, patterns, wooden thimble, needle, and fabric for making the outfits. Another kit came with a 10in (25cm) mannequin doll with movable arms, molded hair and shoes, and painted features. It also came with assorted colored thread, scissors, patterns, metal thimble, needle, and fabric. It also contained felt hats and trim for decorating the hats and dresses. The concept for this mannequin doll was that a child could take it along while traveling and have something to do to pass the time not to mention that it was educational.

Another popular sewing kit was the Stitchcraft Sewing Set, which included a 6-1/2in (17cm) composition doll with moveable arms, molded hair and socks, and painted features. Concord Toys in New York made this set No. 205. The mannequin had a tiny hole in the bottom of one foot probably in order to stand. There were also two wooden embroidery hoops approximately 4-1/8in (11cm) in diameter, seven pieces of fabric with cross stitch designs with one in the hoops. It contained a paper pattern for a coat, six doll dresses, eight wooden clothespins, two thimbles, one piece of tracing paper, and a small amount of embroidery floss.

The Jean Darling Sewing Outfit made by Standard ToyKraft Products Inc. New York was a sewing kit made for girls in 1936. It came with a 6in (15cm) bisque doll, six dresses, three pots with flowers, thread, needles, thimbles, scissors, and three small spools of thread. It came in a 16in x 10-1/2in (41cm x 27cm) bright yellow, red, and blue box. Another set was the Jean Darling Luggage Doll Sewing Kit. This kit was made to look like a suitcase and measured 13-1/2in x 9-1/2in (34 cm x 24cm). The box had great travel graphics on the back and front. The side reads "Copyright 1949 by standard Toykraft Prod, Inc. New York." Inside there was a plastic 6in (15cm) mannequin doll with cutout clothing, thread, needles and scissors.

A different kind of sewing kit was produced in the 50's. It was the Joan Paper Doll Sewing Kit, which had cut outs of dresses that you could trace onto some colorful paper and cut out. It included a sturdy Joan paper doll, punch out dress patterns, colorful paper to cut the dresses from, and a fashion guide booklet.

Left: This photo shows the Little Traveler's Sewing Kit from 1949.

Below: One version of the Little Traveler's Sewing Kit included a 10in (25cm) mannequin and accessories.

The inside of the Little Traveler's Sewing Kit with 10in (25cm) mannequin.

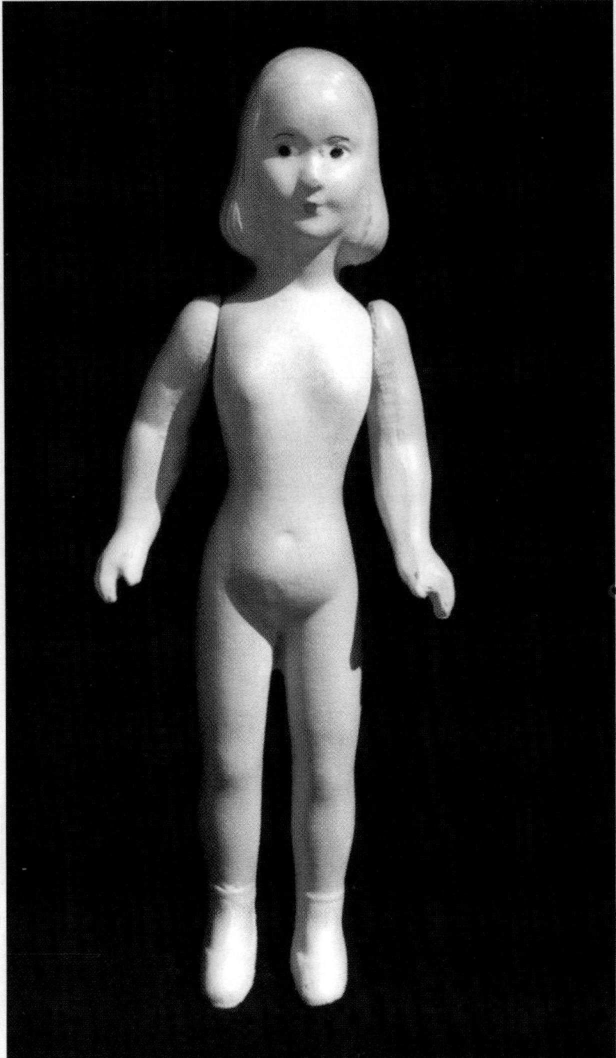

The 10in (25cm) doll from the Little Traveler's Sewing Kit.

The two versions of the Little Traveler's Sewing Kit mannequin. One is 12in (31cm) tall and the other is 6in (15cm) tall.

This Betty doll is from the Little Traveler's Sewing Kit of the 1950's.

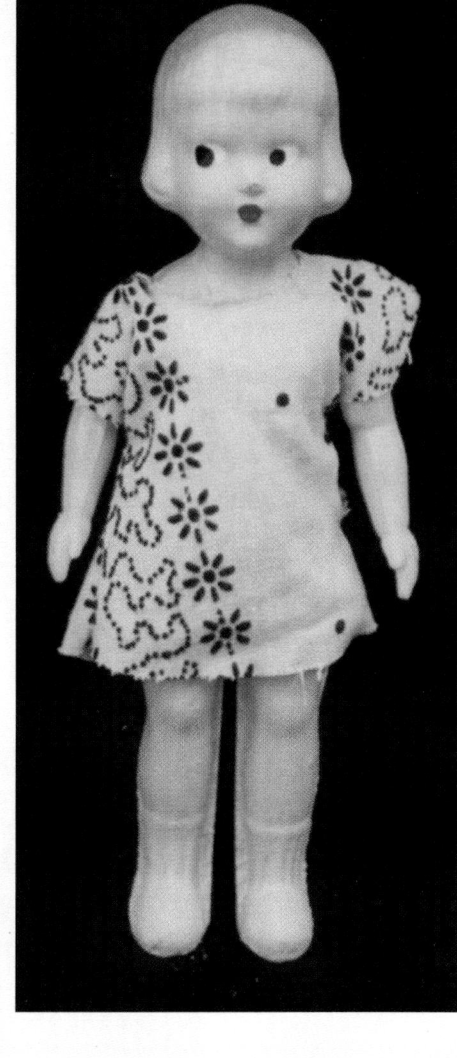

Here is another variation of the Little Traveler's Sewing Kit.

Below: Little Traveler's Sewing Kit with the 6in (15cm) doll and four patterns.

Another version of the Little Traveler's Sewing Kit box with a 6in (15cm) mannequin.

Below: Little Traveler's Sewing Kit with the 6in (15cm) doll also included material, thimble, thread, needle, scissors, and four patterns.

Above: A dressed Collette from the 1950's.

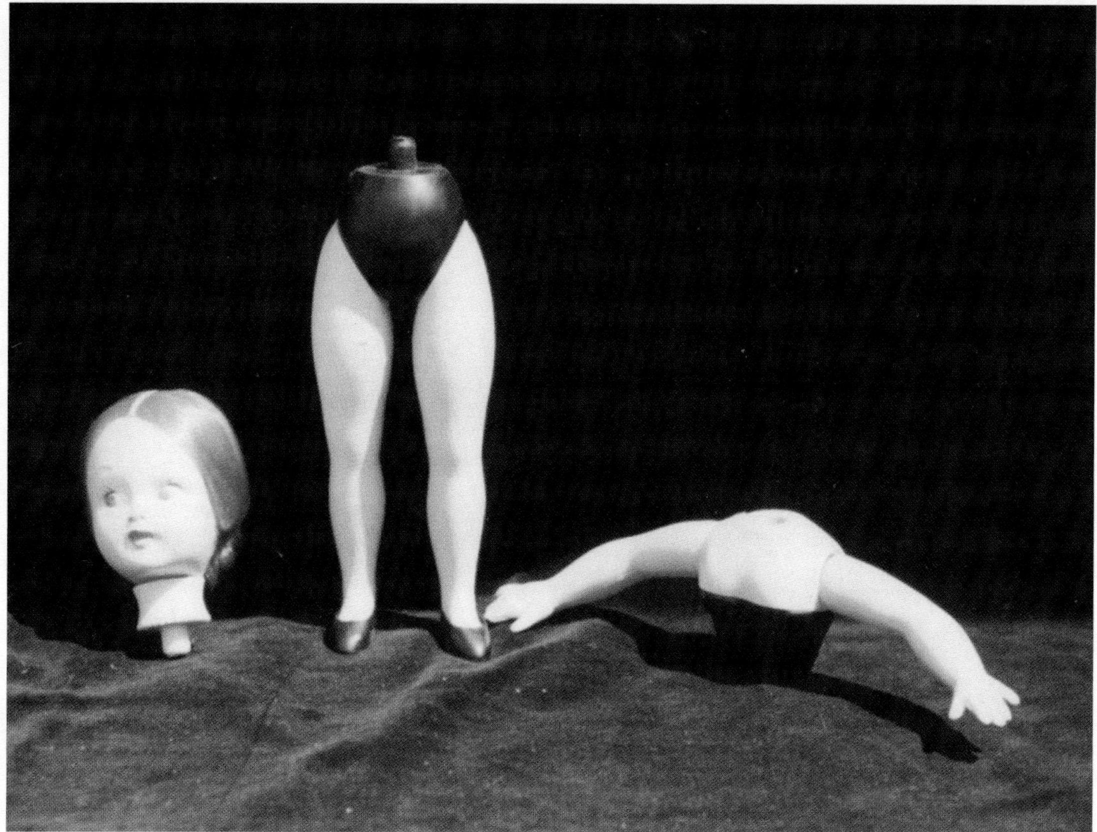

Above: Collette came in piece so that she could be dressed and then snapped together.

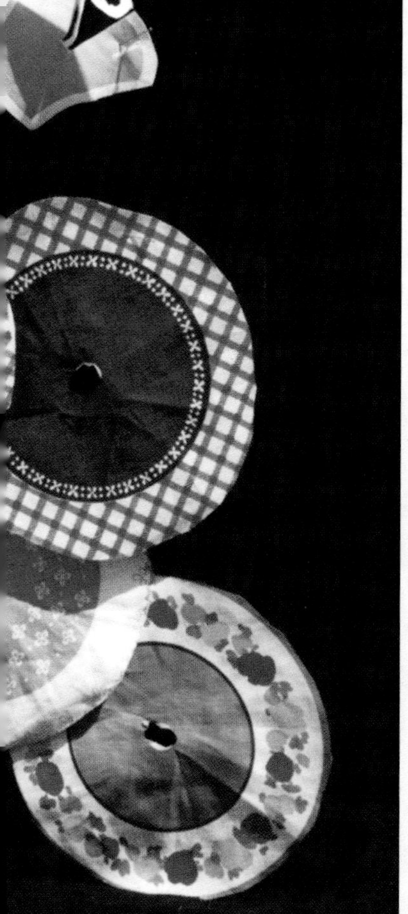

Collette with all her cut out clothes.

The Collette mannequin doll instruction guide.

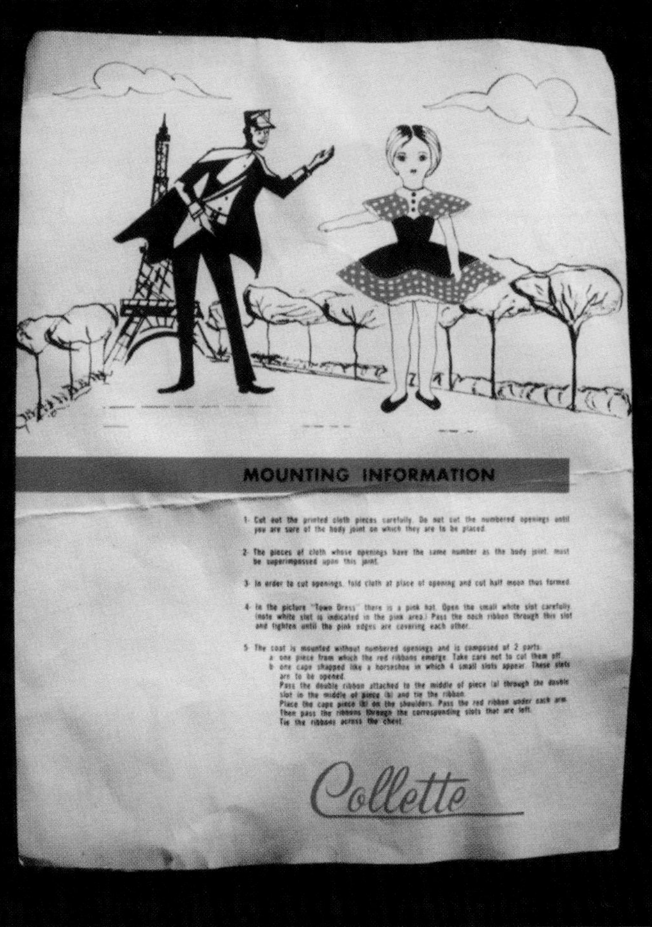

The Collette mannequin mounting information.

This is the small 12-1/2in (32cm) sewing Belinda mannequin. Her arms were not removable. She is wearing a hand-made dress.

These patterns were available for the Belinda mannequin. They are #599, #594, #614, and #620 respectively.

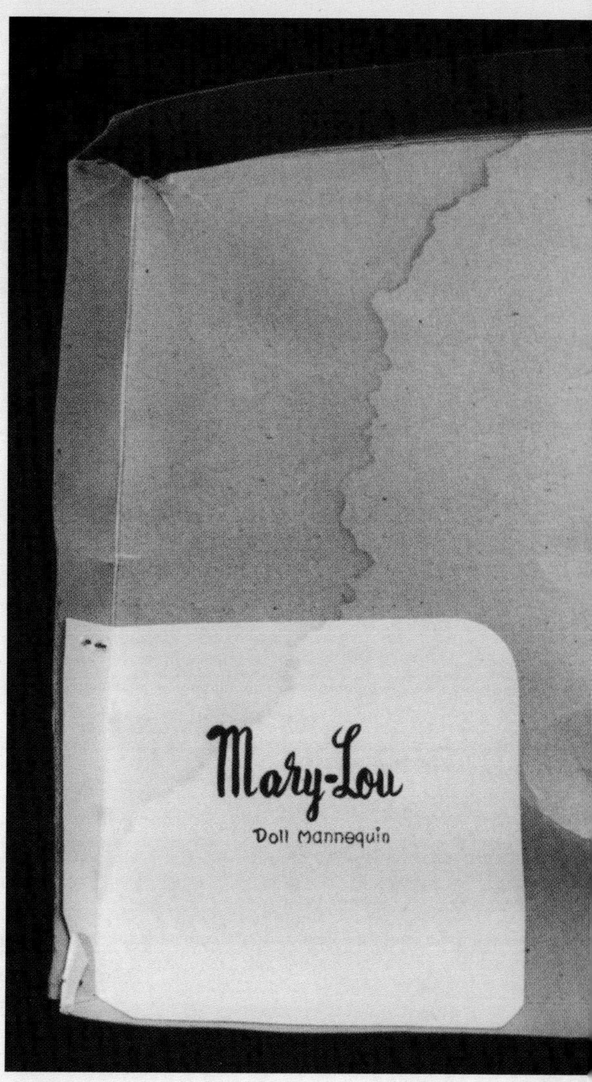

Above: Mary-Lou Doll Mannequin box.

Right: Instructions for dressing your Mary-Lou mannequin.

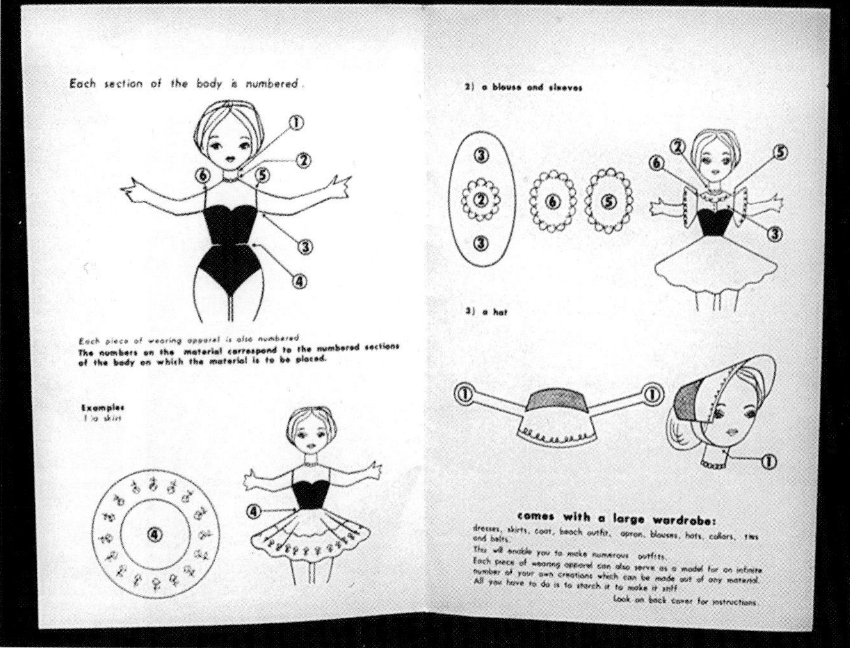

Above: The inside of the Mary-Lou Doll Mannequin from the 1950's.

Right: Another variation of the Mary-Lou mannequin manufactured by Rosko.

Above: This is a 7in (18cm) Lingerie Lou doll with international costumes patterns from the 1950's.

Right: Here are two variations of the Lingerie Lou doll. One is brunette and the other is blonde, but both are ready to be dressed.

Above: This pattern booklet shows how to make 16 international costumes for Lingerie Lou.

Left: This is a pattern for a Spanish-style dress for Lingerie Lou.

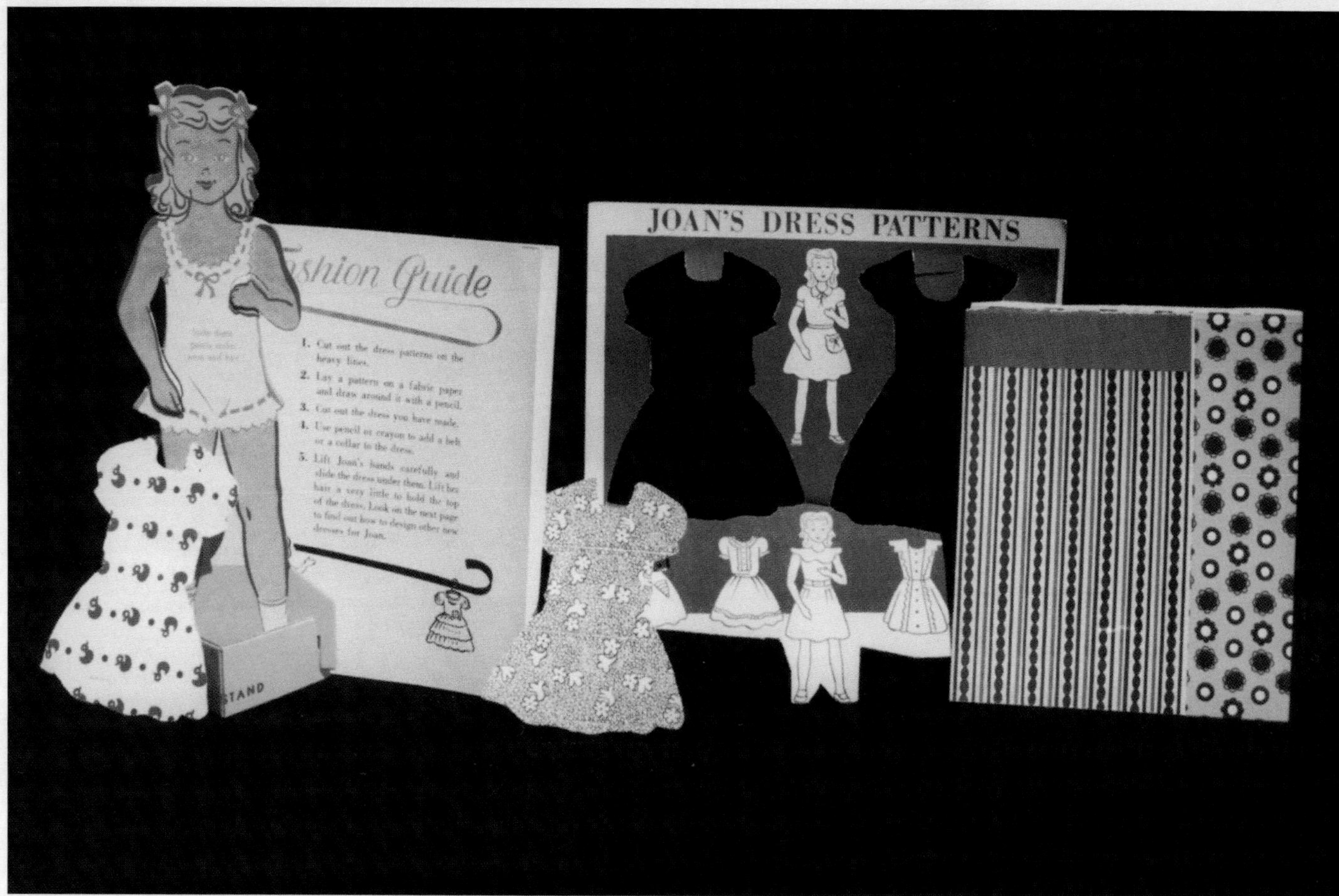

The Joan paper doll came with punch out dresses used as cutting guides on the provided fabric.

Caring for Your Miniature Mannequins

A big part of collecting these mannequins is caring for them. They can be easily damaged if great care is not given to them. I have received many mannequins through the mail that were not packaged correctly and were therefore damaged in transport. Then again, I have received some that were very well packaged that were still damaged. Extreme heat or cold can damage mannequins as well as humidity and sunlight, so it is best to keep them in a dimly lit room with little exposure to heat, cold, humidity, or light. I have included pictures of what the elements and carelessness can do to your mannequins.

Humidity and water can damage the paint and composition of the doll's body. The paint may pucker and peel and the composition material may flake off. A doll can also mildew which is extremely difficult to remove once it imbeds itself into your mannequin.

These dolls can crack easily and crazing is very common on them even in good environments. Crazing is the formation of fine cracks on the body and face of the mannequin doll. Sometimes the crazing is so extreme that the top layer of the doll starts to peel up. Minimal crazing appears as just a small spider vein on the top glazing.

These mannequin dolls were usually painted with flesh tone paint after the mold was finished so it's not unusual to see the paint begin to flake off from extreme exposure to the elements. A green body mold is found under the paint.

The arms of these mannequin dolls are also susceptible to damage when removing them from the doll. If you are not careful in the way that you remove the doll's arms, you can easily crack the shoulder or arm peg of the doll. A small booklet was included in some of the kits that explained how to take the arms off for maximum protection of these dolls. The dolls must also be placed on their stands in the right manner so as not to break one of the legs or feet off which is very easily done. If you decide to dress your mannequin, take the arms off first. Then place the outfit over the head and insert the arms back into the armholes of the outfit. Be sure to push the arms back into the arm sockets. Sometimes you will encounter a mannequin whose arms will not stay in. You can place a small amount of scotch tape around the pegs and then reinsert them. If you have a mannequin with broken limbs, you can either glue them back on with dependable glue or have them professionally repaired if you don't want to have an obviously repaired doll.

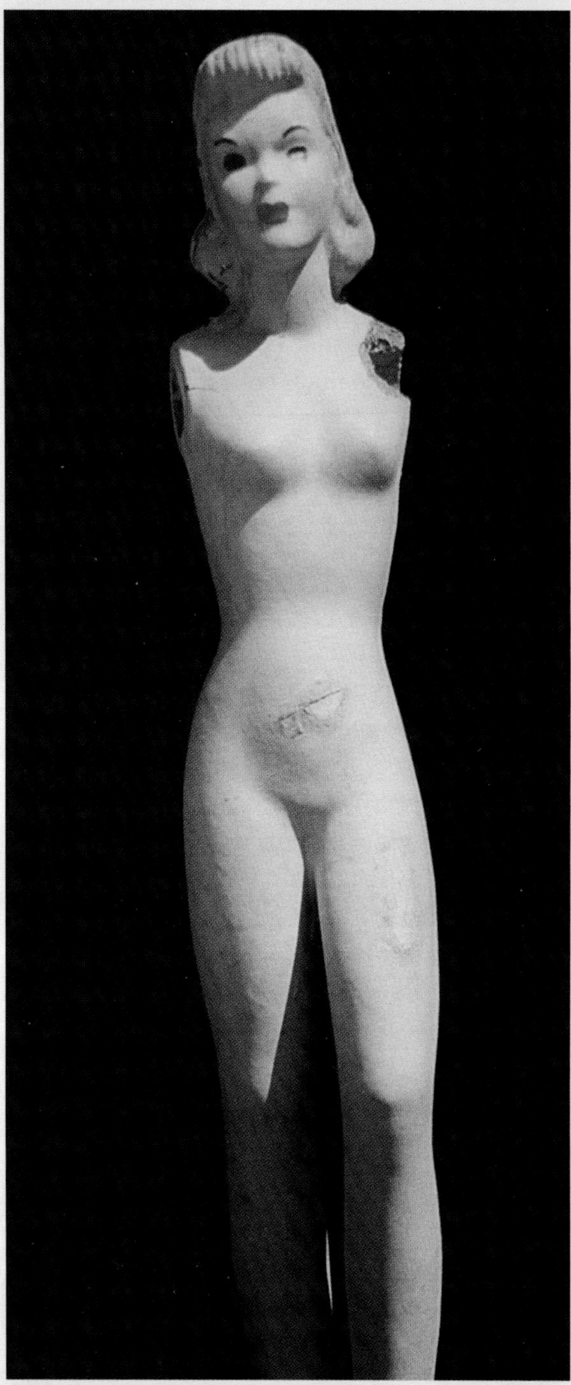

This photo shows what water can do to composition mannequins. Notice how the paint is puckering and peeling on her stomach and right thigh.

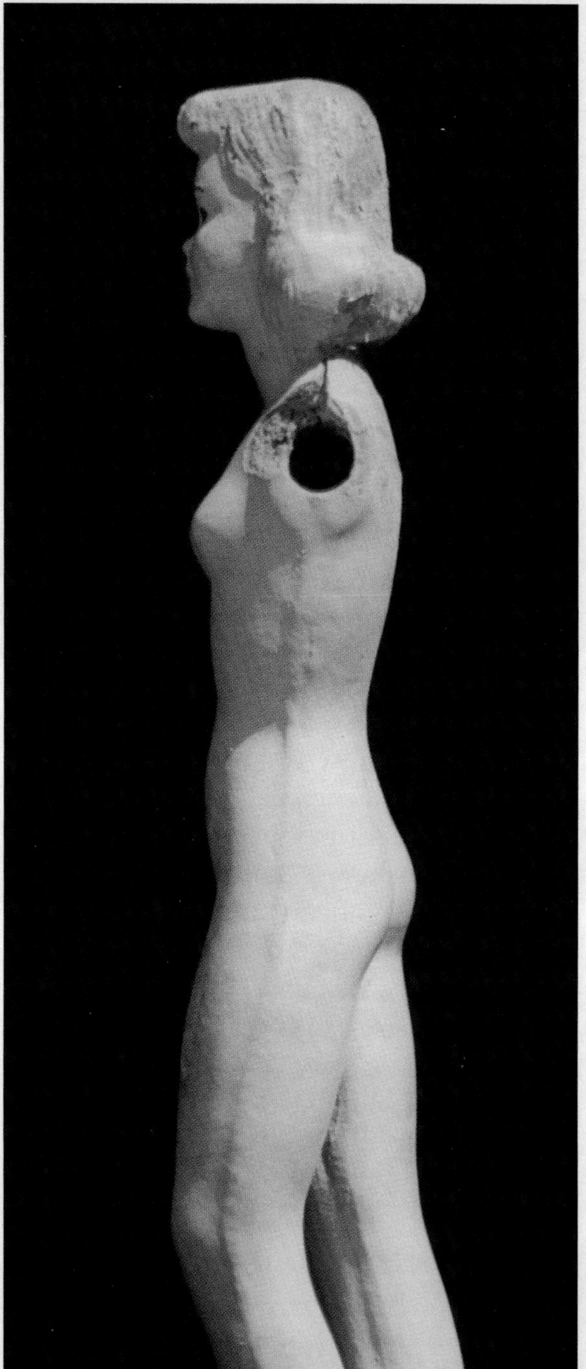

This photo shows how the armhole and hair are peeling off of this mannequin due to water damage.

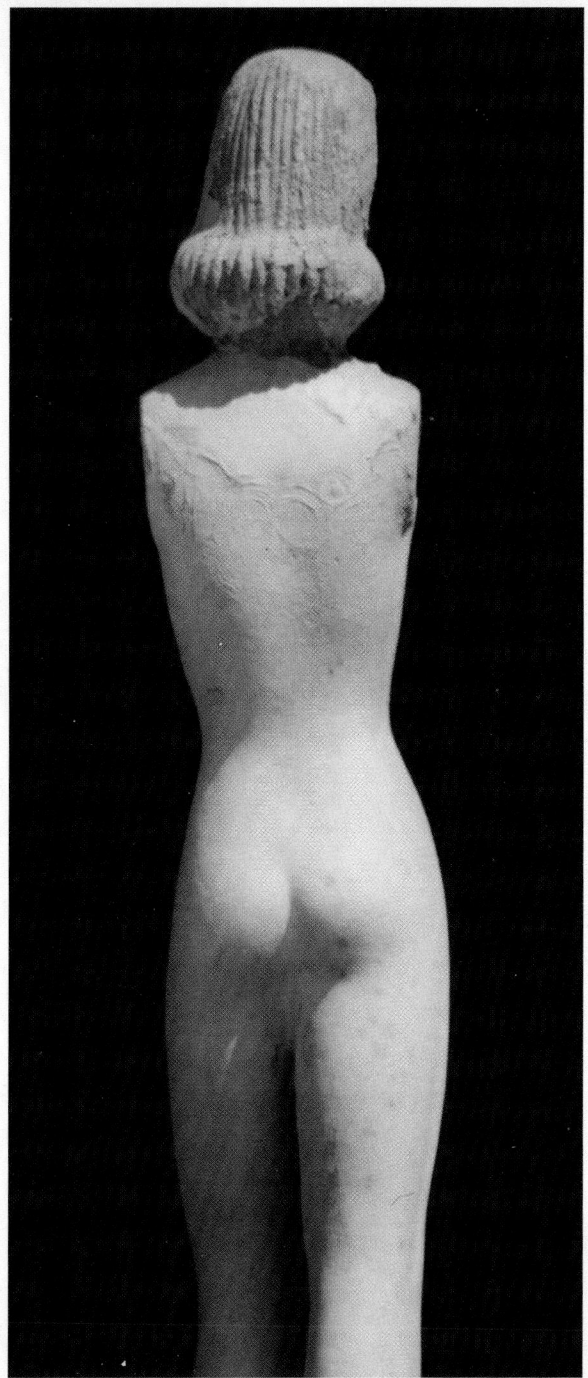

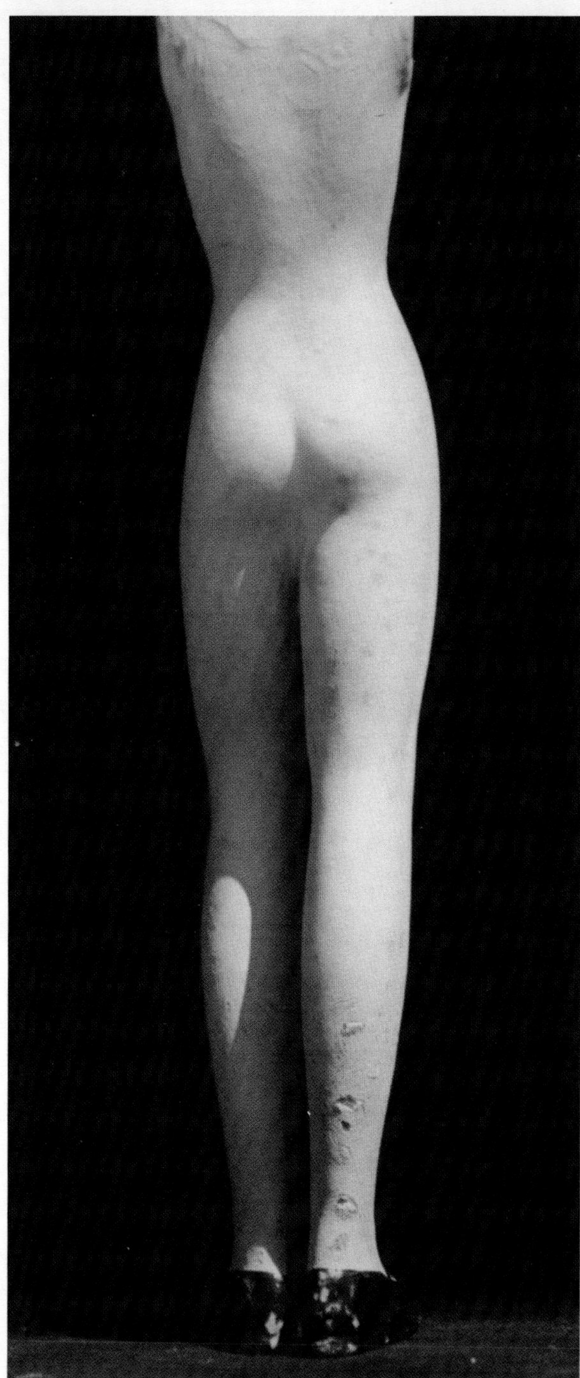

Here you can see the paint puckering due to water damage.

Here there are pieces coming off at the mannequin's ankle and the paint is peeling on her shoe.

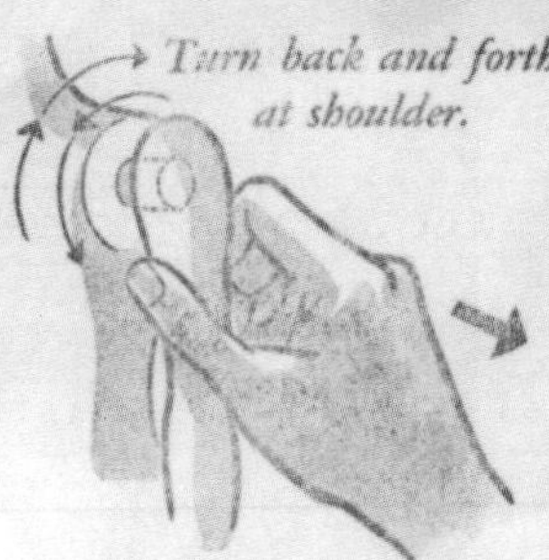

HOW TO REMOVE "Peggy's" ARMS

DON'T!

Do not pull at wrist or arm itself.

Peggy's arms are held in with a peg and socket.

DO!

Turn back and forth at shoulder.

Take the arm at the shoulder, then—with a back and forth circular motion—loosen arm and pull away from body.

SO "PEGGY" WILL STAND...insert the nail into the black spot marked on the wooden block. Several taps with a hammer or other hard object will hold the nail firmly. You will note that "Peggy's" right foot has a hole in the bottom. Place "Peggy" upright on the wooden base so that the nail enters the hole in the foot – and Presto – "Peggy" will stand unassisted.

IMPORTANT NOTICE. Because of prevailing conditions beyond our control, we do not guarantee this mannequin against breakage. However, careful handling will assure you satisfactoty results.

DRITZ-TRAUM COMPANY
Incorporated
11-15 E. 26th St., New York City, N. Y.

This pamphlet on how to remove your mannequin's arms came with the Peggy Mannequin.

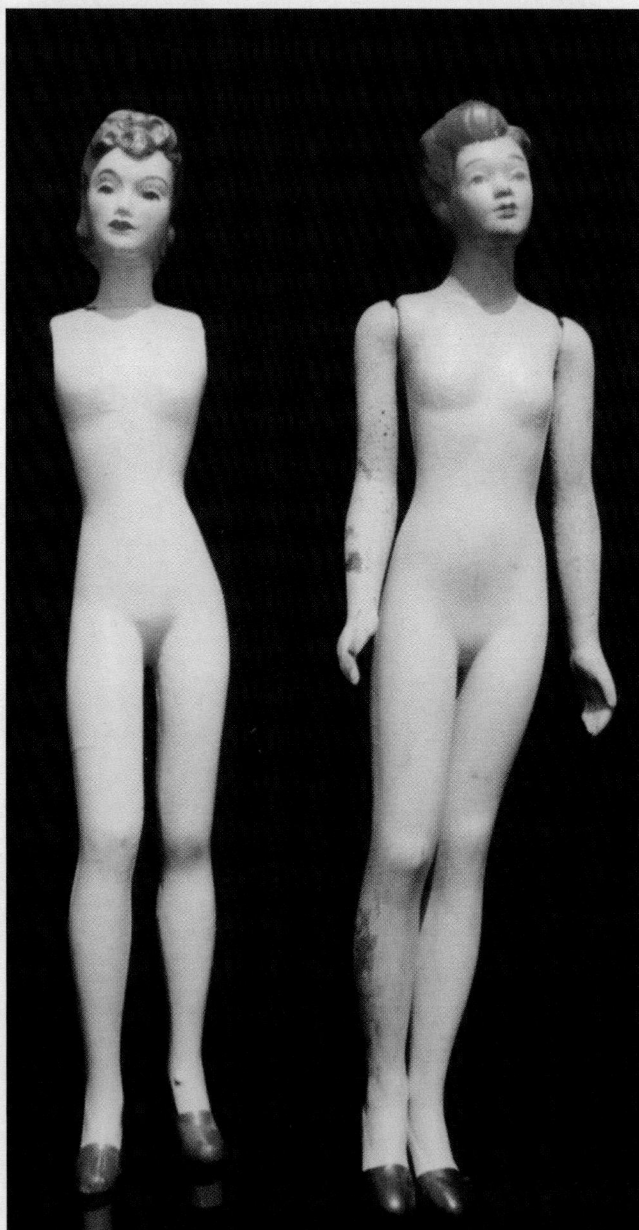

Both of these mannequins are damaged. The one on the left has no arms and has a cracked neck. The other mannequin has water damage on her right arm and leg.

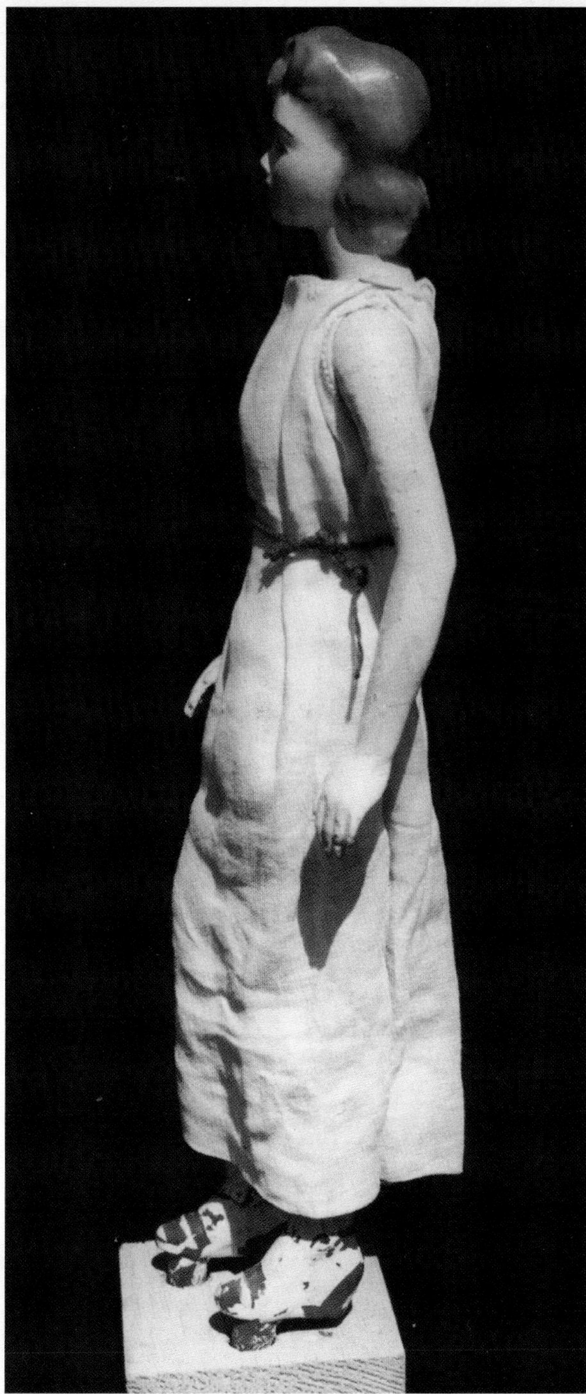

This mannequin's paint has begun flaking off due to exposure to the elements. It is most likely due to water damage.

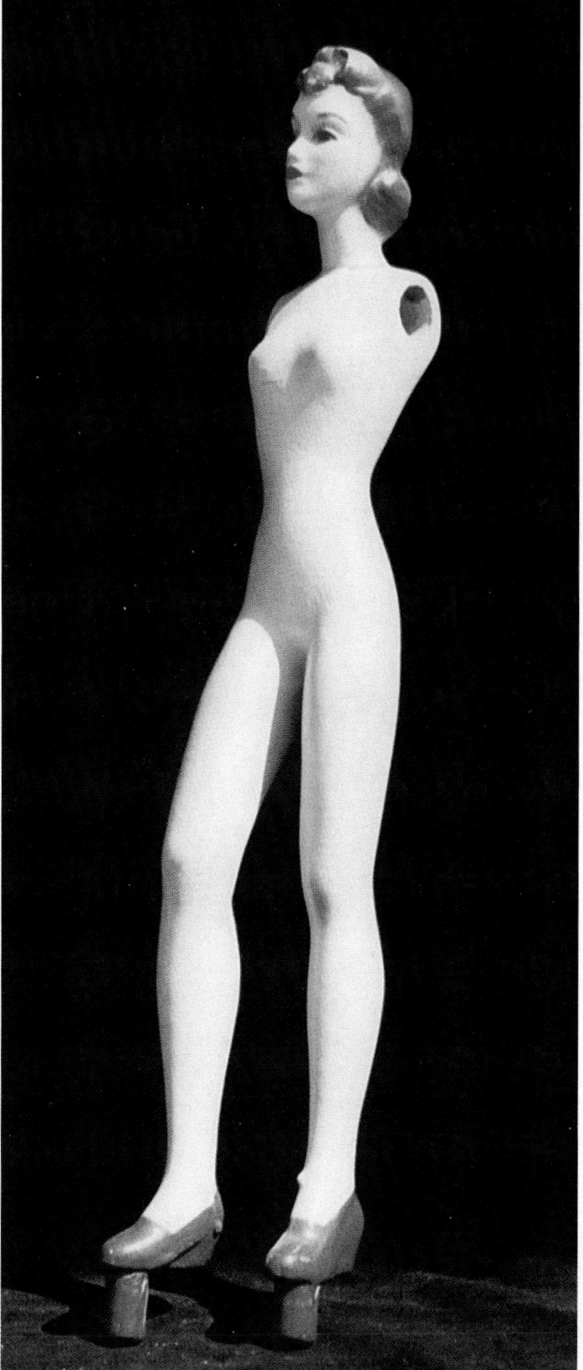

This 12-1/2in (32cm) mannequin has pegs on the bottoms of her feet that fit into her base. You can see that this composition mannequin has removable arms.

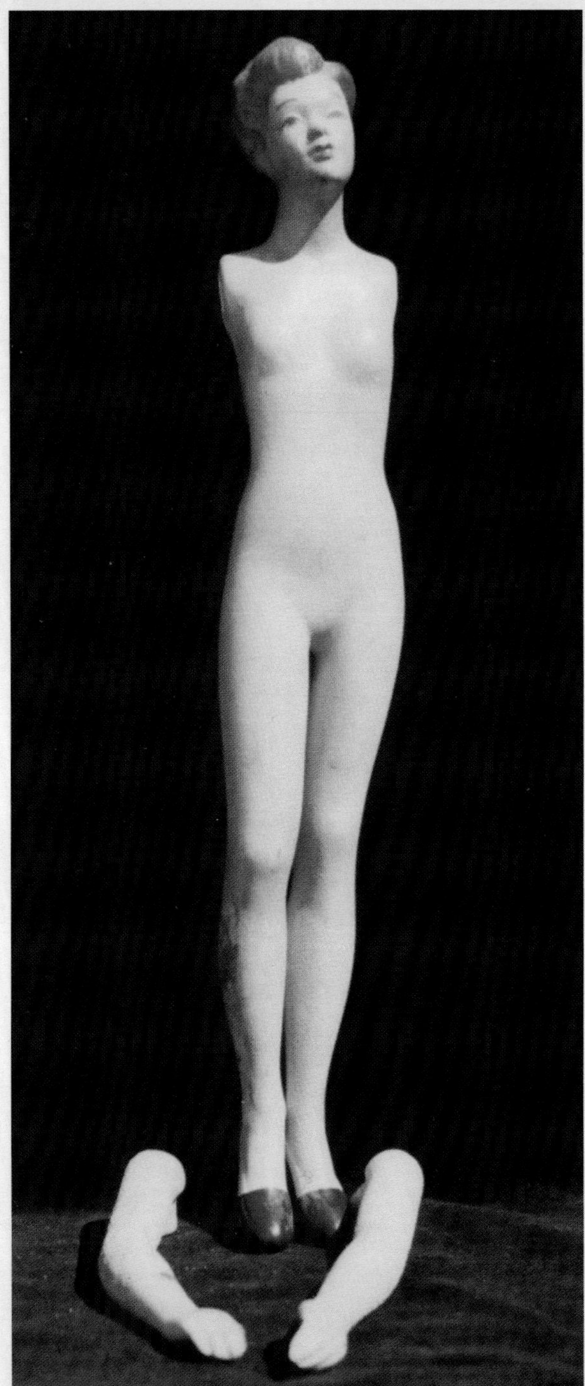

This rubber mannequin has removable arms and painted shoes. However, she does have water damage on her right leg.

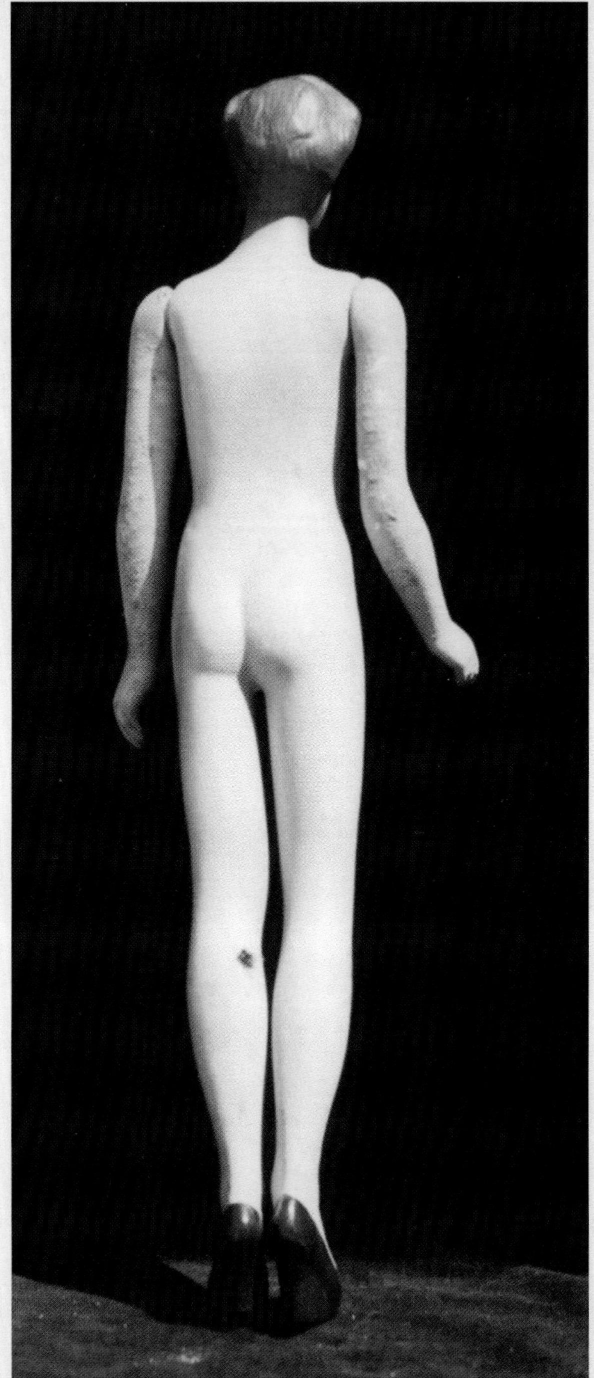

In this photo, you can see that the rubber is peeling off of this rubber miniature mannequin.

Mannequin Patterns

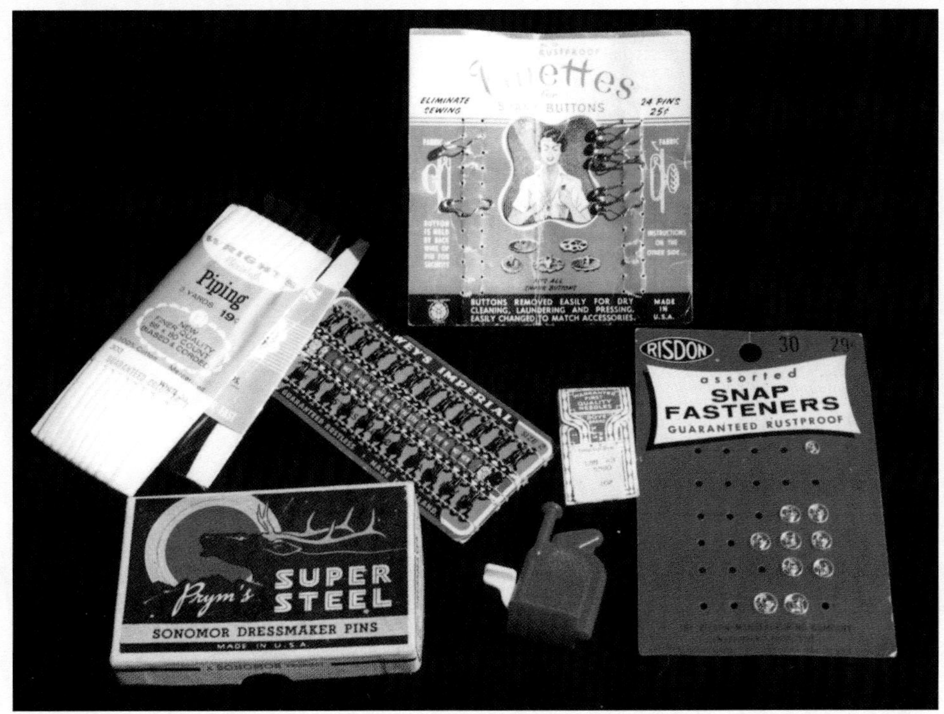

Vintage sewing accessories from the 1940's and 1950's.

One thing that I have noticed since starting to collect these sewing mannequins is that the mannequin patterns can at times command a lot more money than the dolls themselves. I have seen the patterns going for a large amount of money while the loose sewing mannequin dolls command less. I think that maybe their popularity is due to the fact that the 15in (38cm) mannequin patterns will fit the popular fashion dolls such as Gene, Alex, and Tyler with only slight alterations. In addition, the smaller 12-1/2in (32cm) mannequin patterns will fit the 11-1/2in (29cm) doll with very few adjustments. Another reason that I feel that they are so popular is that they are incredibly detailed unlike some of the doll patterns of today which seem somewhat juvenile in concept. I have noticed though, that lately Vogue and Simplicity are beginning to get more elaborate with the patterns that they are producing for the new fashion dolls.

Most of these old mannequin patterns came with the sewing kits that featured the mannequins, but you could also order extra sets by mail to go with your mannequin dolls just by sending in a form that was in the kit. The extra patterns came three to a set and cost between 19¢ and 25¢, and they came in a wide range of styles and fashion such as daywear, evening wear, underwear, and bridal wear. The early Simplicity mannequin patterns had "Exclusively for Latexture Products, Inc." printed across the bottom while the later one had "Exclusively for Fashiondol" printed on the bottom. Simplicity seems to have made the most sewing mannequin patterns, followed by McCall. You can also find the bigger patterns that came out to fit the McCall Margit Nilsen mannequin dolls, or the other bigger display dolls. Some were made by Butterick and are labeled "Minnekin Pattern" in red ink under the Butterick name on the front of the pattern. There is no size given, just a pattern number and a picture of the outfit. You have to be very careful in handling most of these old patterns since they are about 50 years old and are very brittle. To preserve your patterns, make a copy of the patterns

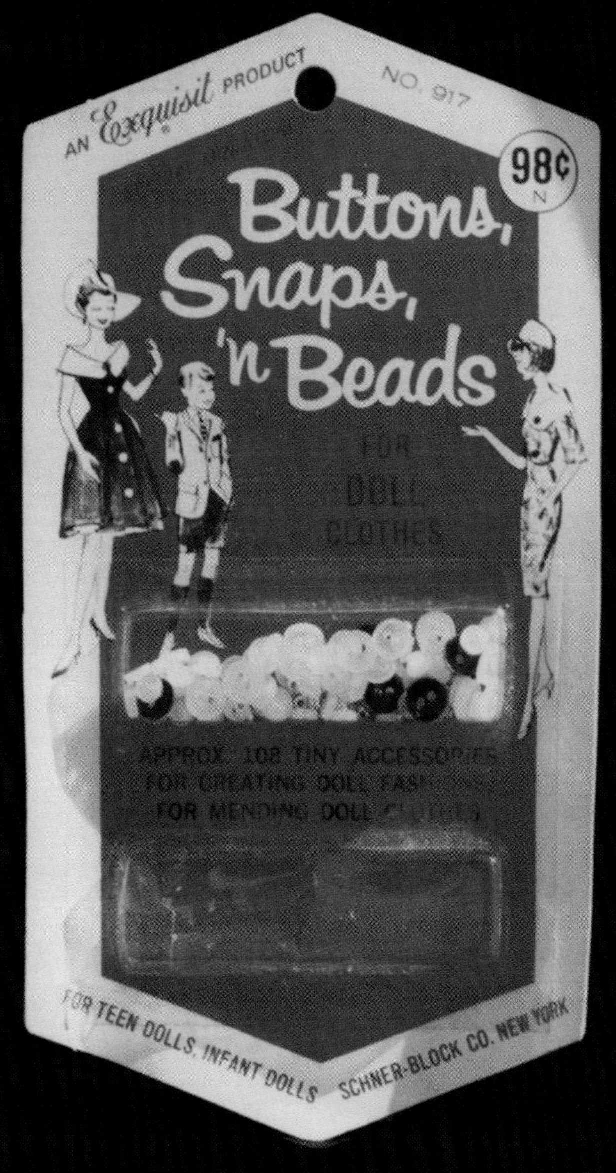

These are sewing accessories made especially for doll clothing.

To All Young Would-be Stylists

This is a mannequin, not an ordinary doll. She is a miniature of a teen-age girl, made of a plastic material, but not flexible.

Because the War Production Program requires rubber which we previously used in the manufacture of these mannequins, we are now using a new material to continue making them so that you can do your bit by learning to sew and save.

Important:—To attach the arms, insert the pegs of the arms into the armholes with a backward and forward twisting motion as you press them in. When putting the pegs of the feet into the base, a slight pressure will bring them together to fit the holes in the base. Do not use force.

If you follow these directions, the mannequin will last indefinitely to model the dresses you make for her.

Save all the patterns. You can make many more dresses from the sets which are available by interchanging the blouses, skirts, and sleeves. Use your ingenuity in combining materials, or in making different accessories such as collars, belts, etc., and in using both prints and plain materials. Buttons, trimmings and ribbons will also give variety.

Learn this way to plan a complete wardrobe. We know you will have a lot of fun.

For replacements of arms, send to the address below. Be sure to say whether right or left arm is required. To cover cost of postage and handling, send 13c in stamps for one—23c for a pair.

Patterns Available for 12½" Mannequins

Set A — Pinafore
Slip & Panties
Nurse's Cape

Set B — Play Dress
Evening Dress
Pajamas

Set C — Housecoat
Skirt & Blouse
Bathing Suit

Set D — Easy-to-Make Dress
Nurse's Uniform
Daytime Dress

19c for Each Set of 3

LATEXTURE PRODUCTS, INC. 17 Rose St., New York City

This guide allowed a person to order more patterns for their Simplicity mannequin and told how to care for her.

and do not handle the originals if at all possible. You can usually find these patterns on the Internet auction sites or at antique shops.

You will have to hunt under Mannequin, "Minikin," "Minnekin," or "Minnikin" on the Internet auction sites. I have searched under all of those spellings and have found a treasure trove of items under each. You can also look under the pattern section. Just be sure to watch carefully—sometimes the patterns are listed under women's vintage patterns. I look at as many as I can in a few hours. Be prepared to spend a great deal of your time online if that is the route that you choose to take. It requires diligence and perseverance to find what you want, but if you are willing to spend the time and energy it takes online or hunting through the antique shops, you can discover some great treasures. I have amassed a large collection of my own doing just that.

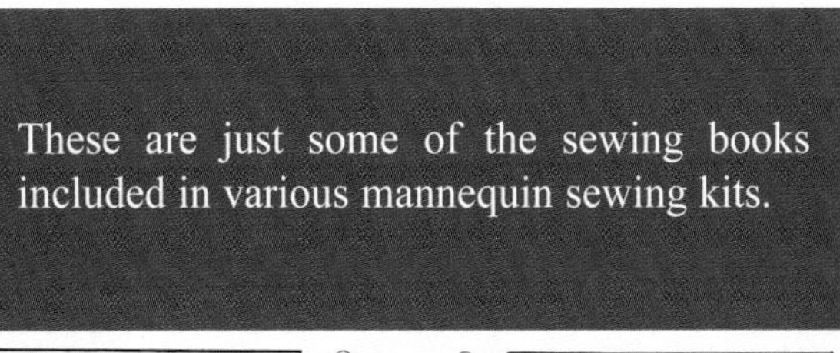

These are just some of the sewing books included in various mannequin sewing kits.

ROLL YOUR OWN

Scarf Hat

With a soft, stretchable, but firm scarf, 24 inches square, you can have a new hat every time your heart desires. The kerchief or square scarf may be of print or plain. Brico Lifetime Scarfs which are on sale for 25c at Woolworth's have lovely floral and paisley designs. Here are two easy styles to roll that make a refreshing change from wearing your scarf in traditional peasant style.

Band-Up Turban: 1. Lay the scarf on a table and fold into a triangle. 2. Fold the left hand corner of the triangle over, bringing the point on the right side of the triangle. 3. Fold the right hand corner to the same point on the other side. This leaves a small triangular opening at the bottom. 4. Starting at the top, roll the points down together tightly. 5. Stop rolling when it is seven inches from the bottom. 6. Holding the roll in place with the right hand, slip the thumb of the left hand into the triangular opening and turn the whole thing inside out, tucking the rolled ends into the corners. The diagonal opening is worn in front just behind your bewitching bangs or curls. The bump should form a straight ridge across the forehead, with a point at each side giving a pompadour effect.

Elfin Rollers: 1. Lay the scarf on a table and fold into a triangle with the point down. 2. Bring the right point over to the left of the apex. 3. Swing the left corner across in the same manner. 4. Roll the crossed points up to about 7 inches from the top. 5. Turn the hat over and roll up the apex points until the roll is even and smooth all around. Wear on the back of your head.

LATEXTURE PRODUCTS, INC., 17 ROSE STREET, NEW YORK, N. Y.

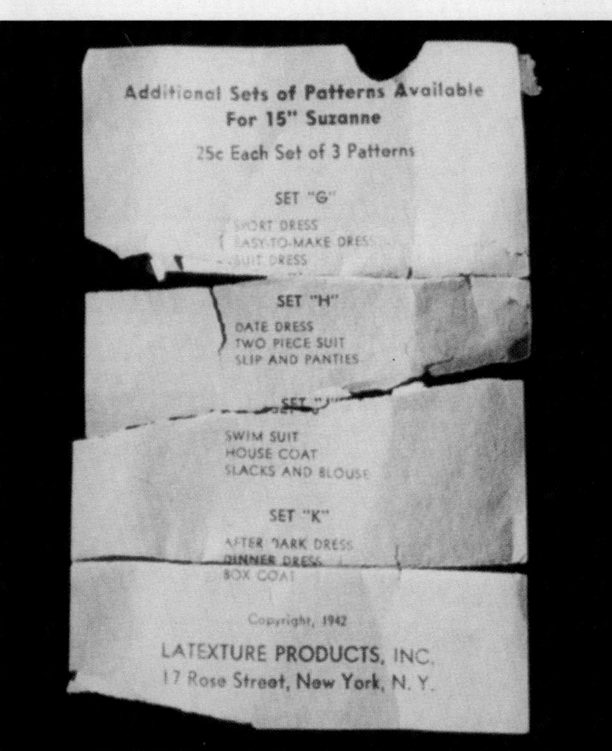

Additional Sets of Patterns Available
For 15" Suzanne

25c Each Set of 3 Patterns

SET "G"
SPORT DRESS
EASY-TO-MAKE DRESS
SUIT DRESS

SET "H"
DATE DRESS
TWO PIECE SUIT
SLIP AND PANTIES

SET "J"
SWIM SUIT
HOUSE COAT
SLACKS AND BLOUSE

SET "K"
AFTER DARK DRESS
DINNER DRESS
BOX COAT

Copyright, 1942

LATEXTURE PRODUCTS, INC.
17 Rose Street, New York, N. Y.

Above Left: This booklet came with the Simplicity mannequin kit.

Above: The back of this "Hints for the Young Designer" booklet shows how to make a scarf. It is a Simplicity sewing guide.

Left: These instructions told how to order more patterns for the 15in (38cm) Suzanne the Mannequin Doll.

Left: The McCall "Tricks in Sewing" booklet.

Below: This shows the inside of the McCall booklet form the 1940's.

Fabric Comes Next

Here are a few simple rules which will help you in selecting your fabric:

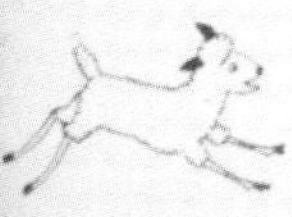

1. Look for labels or ask questions about the fabric you are considering:
   a. Does it wash and how should it be washed — or does it dry clean?
   b. Is it color fast to washing and light?
   c. Is it durable?
   d. Does it wrinkle easily?
   e. Does it retain its shape?
2. Find out how wide the fabric is.

3. Check the number of yards you need, on the back of the pattern envelope. Order the amount of material given under your size, the view you choose and the width of the fabric.

Pick a fabric you like and then get started!

ALTERATION HINTS

FOR ROUND SHOULDERS
Try to square them up yourself. But you can help make your dresses fit better. Just take a small dart from the middle of each shoulder seam down the back.

FOR FLAT CHEST
It's easy to make the adjustment for this very common figure fault. Simply raise the front bodice to a comfortable fit and recut the neckline as shown.

FOR FULL BUSTLINE
After adjusting your bodice pattern to your figure, you'll find the front piece is longer than the back. Make a dart at either side at the underarm seam.

The McCall pattern included with Peggy the Mannequin.

A 1949 pattern for the Peggy the Mannequin Doll.

This McCall pattern was also included with the Peggy the Mannequin Doll.

This McCall pattern was made for the 12-1/2in (32cm) Peggy the Mannequin Doll.

Pattern #4351, made by Butterick, was produced for the bigger display mannequins.

Another Minnekin pattern #5228 for the miniature display mannequins by Butterick.

This Minnekin pattern #4907 was used to dress the store display mannequin. A larger version could be bought for an adult woman.

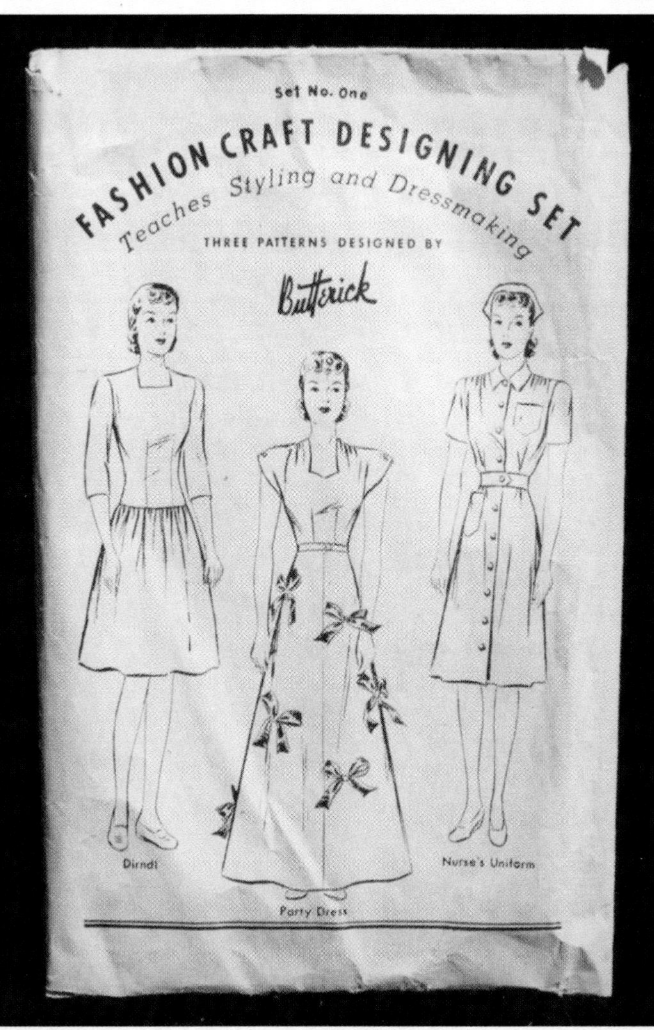

This pattern came with Fashion Craft Designing Set No. One. It showed how to make a dirndl dress, a party dress, and a nurse's uniform.

This Butterick pattern came with the Junior Miss Designer Set.

The pattern one on the left was one of the first mannequin patterns produced for Butterick mannequin sets. Notice how similar they are to one another; however, the one has a nurse's uniform while the other has a bridal gown.

This is a pattern for the 12-1/2in (32cm) Suzanne the Mannequin Doll. The pattern number is #303.

This is an open view of a Suzanne the Mannequin Doll pattern from 1949.

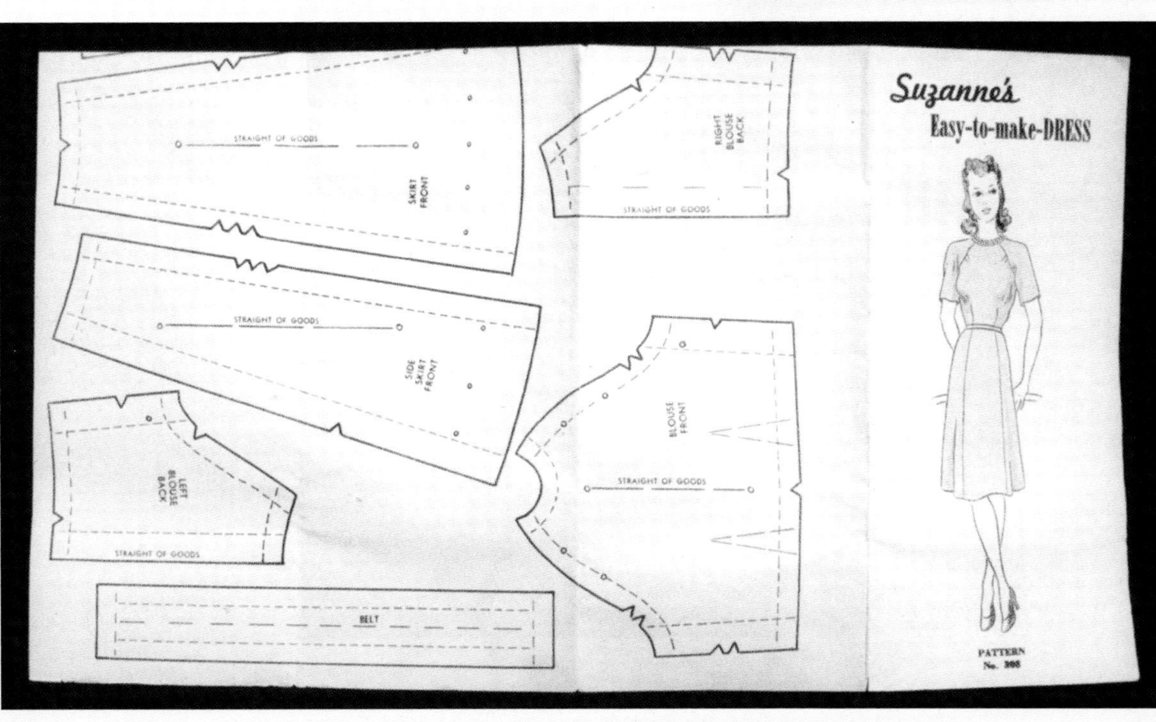

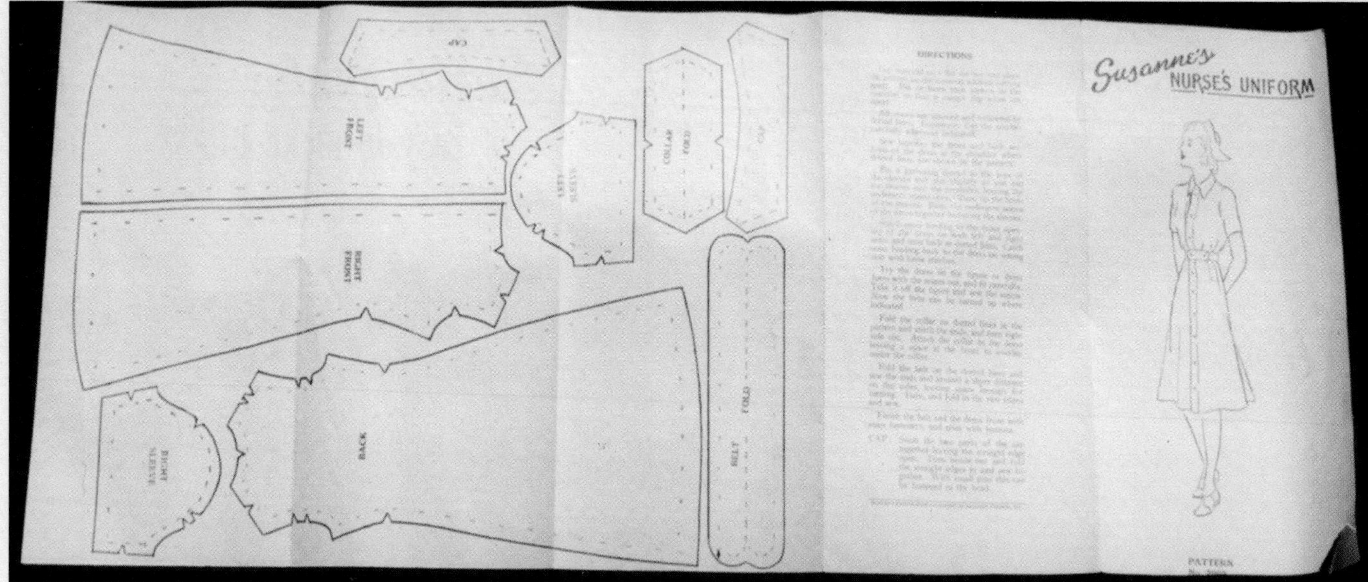

This is a nurse's uniform pattern 2002 that fit the 12-1/2in (32cm) Suzanne the Mannequin Doll.

This set is also for Suzanne the Mannequin Doll. The day time dress pattern on the right has Jan. 21, 1942 written in the corner.

All of these patterns were made to fit the 12-1/2in (32cm) Marianne Mannequin Doll.

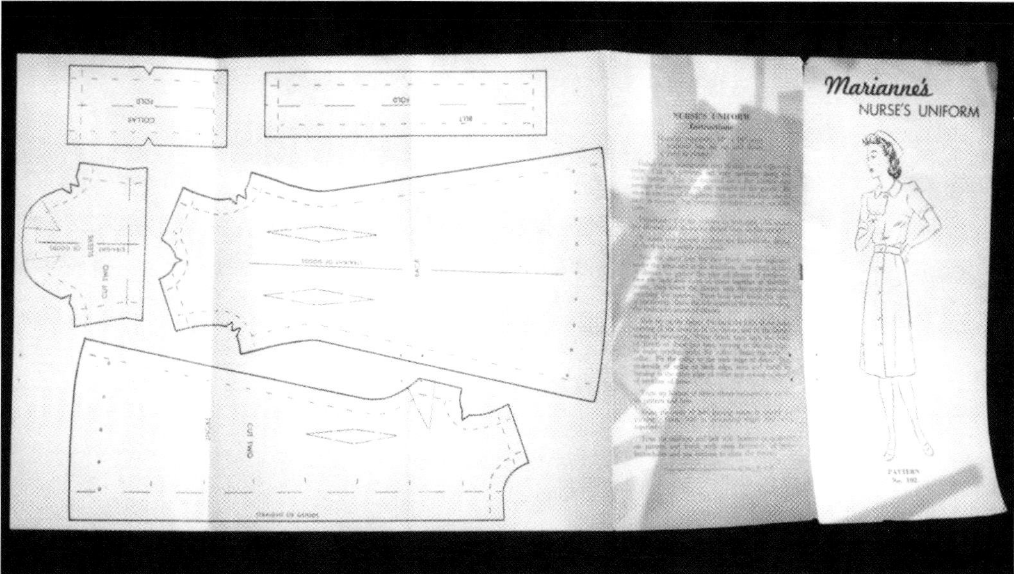

This is an open view of Marianne's nurse's uniform pattern from 1949.

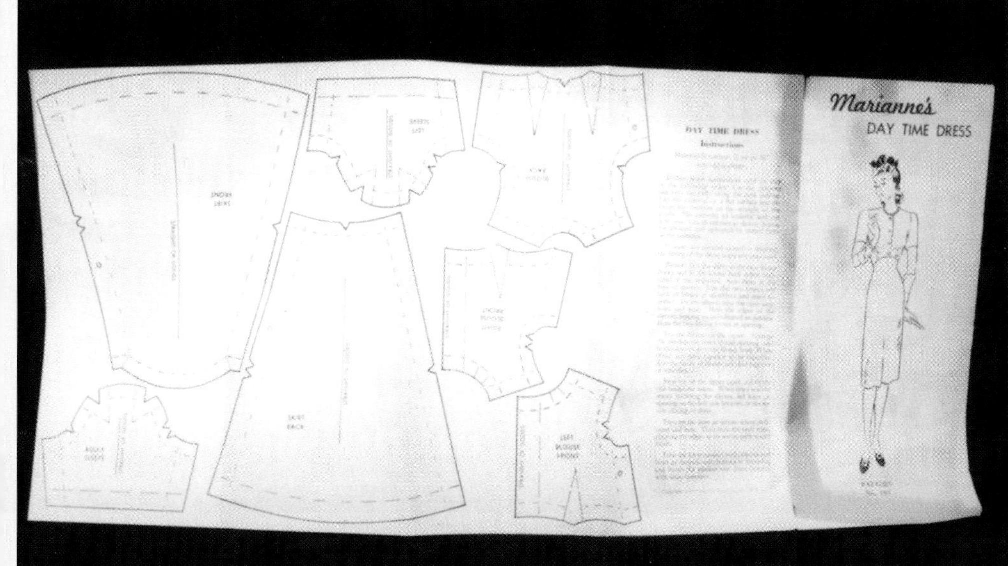

This shows Marianne's day time dress pattern.

These were extra patterns that could be ordered for the 12-1/2in (32cm) Simplicity mannequins. The pattern numbers are 4496, 4977, and 4965 respectively.

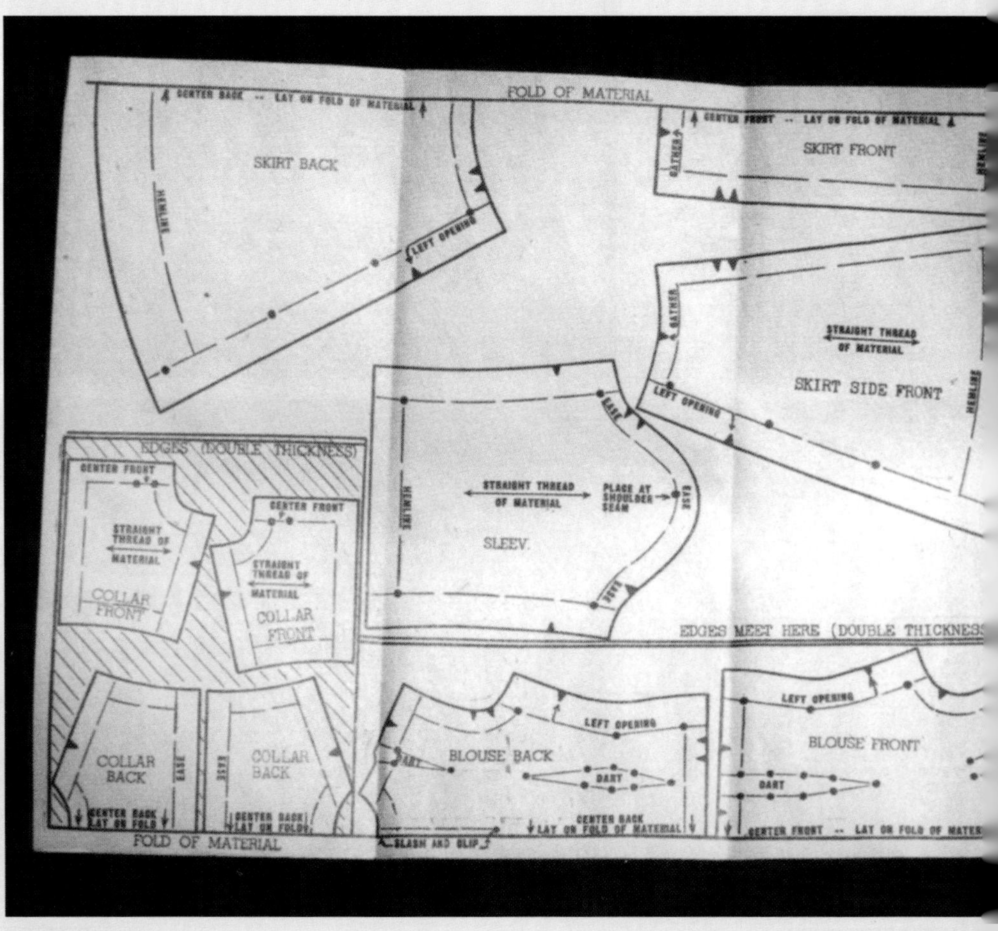

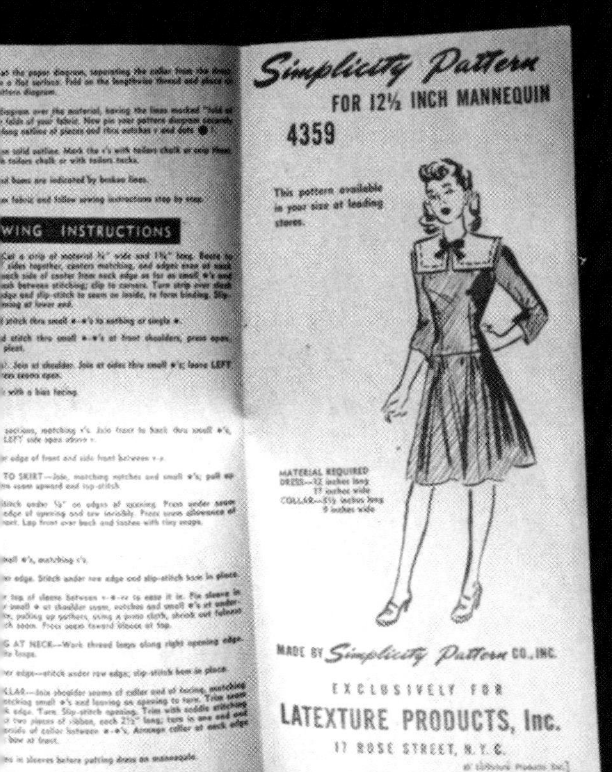

Above: These were also patterns for the 12-1/2in (32cm) Simplicity mannequin.

This is an open view of Simplicity pattern #4359 for the 12-1/2in (32cm) mannequin.

These Simplicity patterns fit the 15in (38cm) mannequin. The pattern numbers are 4980, 4981, and 4984.

Below: This complete open view shows a pattern for the 15in (38cm) Simplicity mannequin.

Below Right: These three Simplicity patterns could be ordered for the 15in (38cm) mannequin in 1949.

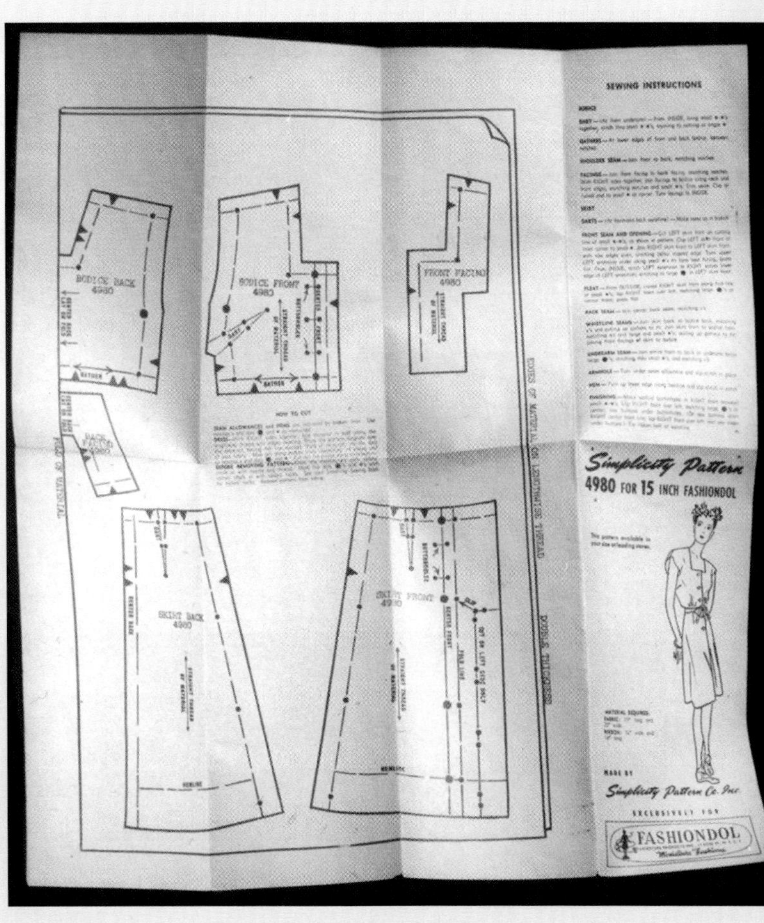

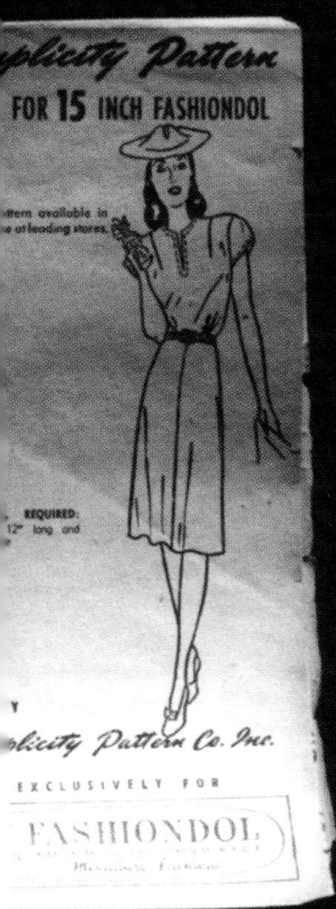

These patterns also fit the 15in (38cm) Simplicity mannequin.

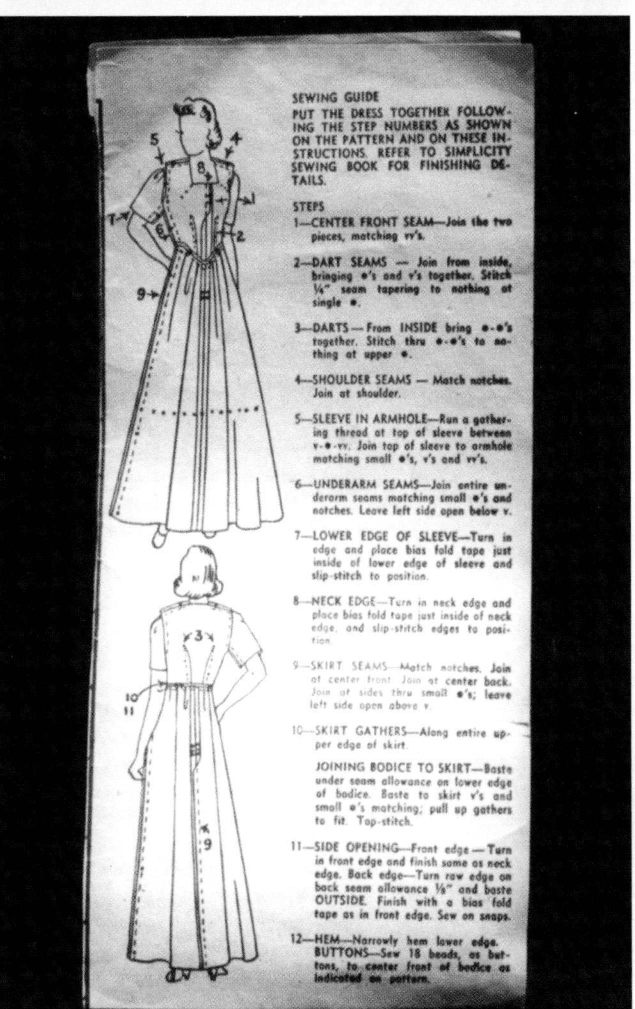

SEWING GUIDE

PUT THE DRESS TOGETHER FOLLOWING THE STEP NUMBERS AS SHOWN ON THE PATTERN AND ON THESE INSTRUCTIONS. REFER TO SIMPLICITY SEWING BOOK FOR FINISHING DETAILS.

STEPS

1—CENTER FRONT SEAM—Join the two pieces, matching vv's.

2—DART SEAMS — Join from inside, bringing •'s and v's together. Stitch ¼" seam tapering to nothing at single •.

3—DARTS — From INSIDE bring •-•'s together. Stitch thru •-•'s to nothing at upper •.

4—SHOULDER SEAMS — Match notches. Join at shoulder.

5—SLEEVE IN ARMHOLE—Run a gathering thread at top of sleeve between v-•-vv. Join top of sleeve to armhole matching small •'s, v's and vv's.

6—UNDERARM SEAMS—Join entire underarm seams matching small •'s and notches. Leave left side open below v.

7—LOWER EDGE OF SLEEVE—Turn in edge and place bias fold tape just inside of lower edge of sleeve and slip-stitch to position.

8—NECK EDGE—Turn in neck edge and place bias fold tape just inside of neck edge, and slip-stitch edges to position.

9—SKIRT SEAMS—Match notches. Join at center front. Join at center back. Join at sides thru small •'s; leave left side open above v.

10—SKIRT GATHERS—Along entire upper edge of skirt.

JOINING BODICE TO SKIRT—Baste under seam allowance on lower edge of bodice. Baste to skirt v's and small •'s matching; pull up gathers to fit. Top-stitch.

11—SIDE OPENING—Front edge — Turn in front edge and finish same as neck edge. Back edge—Turn raw edge on back seam allowance ⅛" and baste OUTSIDE. Finish with a bias fold tape as in front edge. Sew on snaps.

12—HEM—Narrowly hem lower edge. BUTTONS—Sew 18 beads, as buttons, to center front of bodice as indicated on pattern.

The back of pattern 4065 gives instructions on how to construct the outfit.

This shows an Early Nineteenth Century costume for the 12in (31cm) mannequin doll.

This pattern is for a Civil War period costume for the 12in (31cm) mannequin doll.

This pattern is for a 17th Century costume.

Here is an American Revolution costume pattern for the 12in (31cm) mannequin doll.

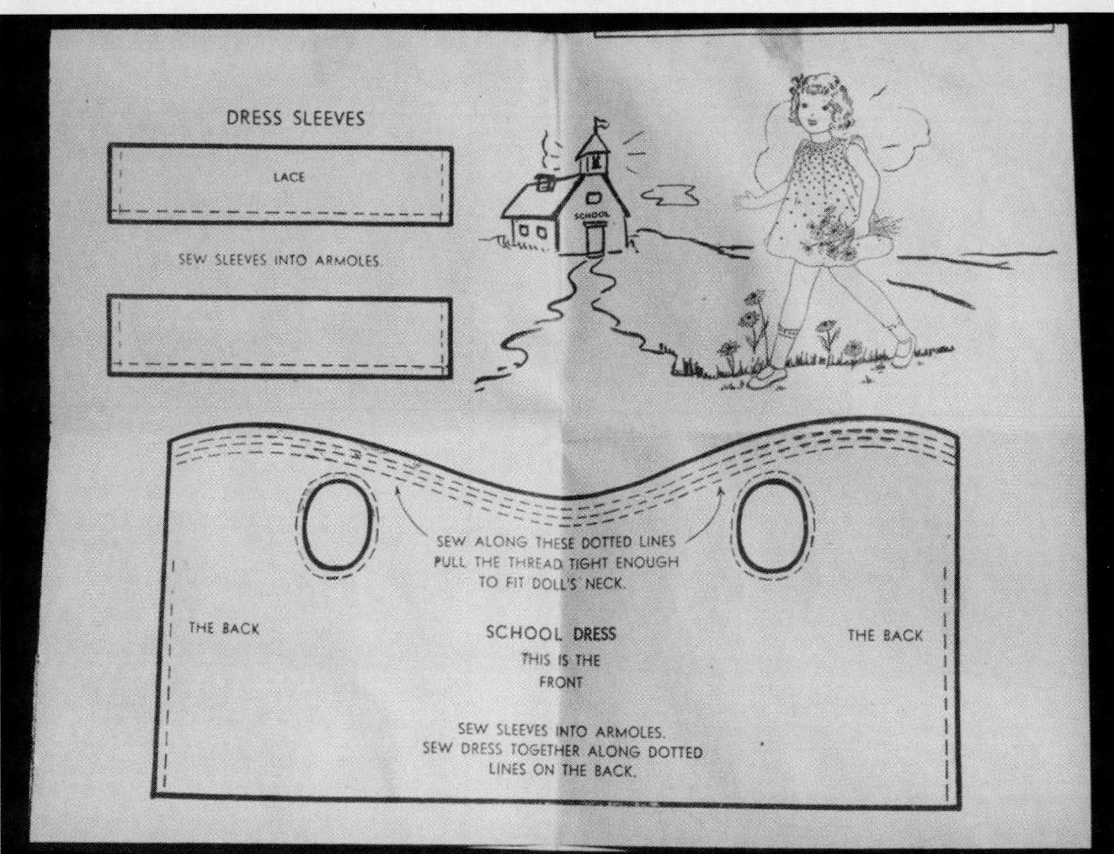

This is one the Little Traveler's Sewing Kit patterns from 1949. It is for the 6in (15cm) mannequin.

This pattern came with the Marie Osmond mannequin doll.

Here are some of the fruits of such patterns. These are hand-made outfits for miniature mannequins.

Some more hand-made outfits for miniature mannequins.

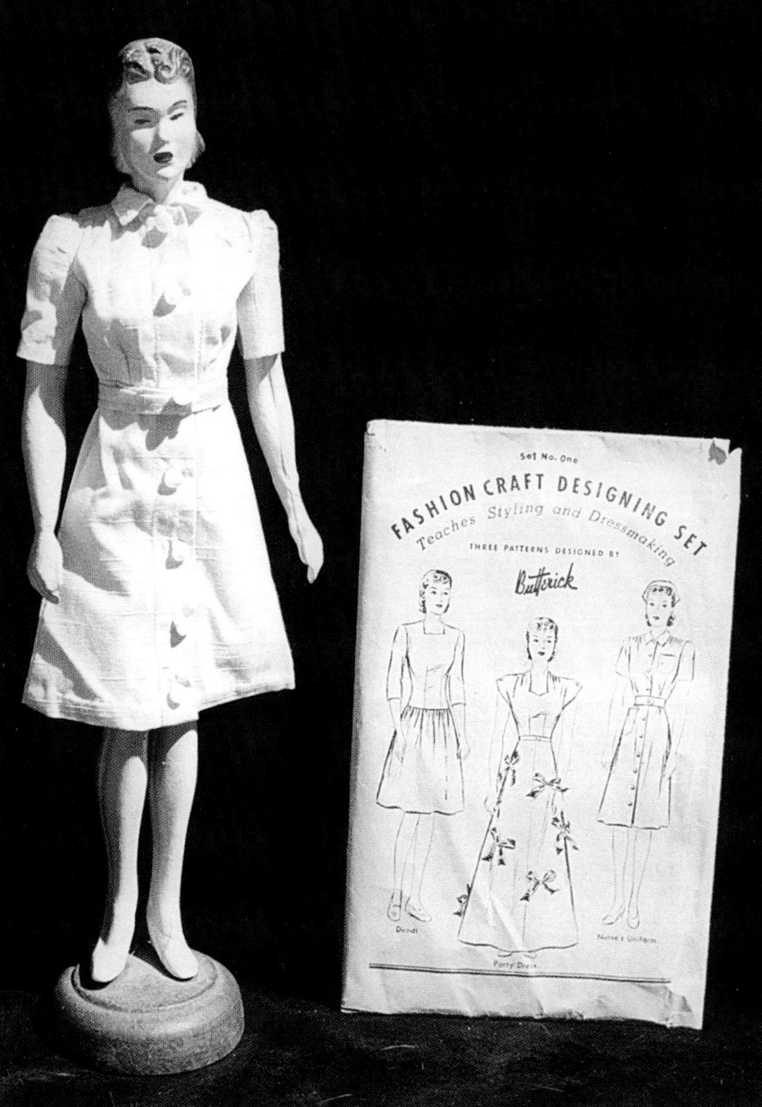

Here is a Junior Miss Butterick mannequin wearing a nurse's uniform made from the pattern on the right.

This 15in (38cm) Suzanne the Mannequin Doll is wearing a home-made gown.

This home-made dress was made from the pattern on the right for a 15in (38cm) Suzanne the Mannequin Doll.

Both of these McCall Peggy mannequins are wearing home-made dresses from McCall patterns. The mannequin on the left is an original mannequin. Notice the bigger arms and the different face paint from the mannequin on the right.

This Peggy mannequin wears a dress made from pattern 6600-1.

Mannequins in the Doll World

Mannequins have also played a big part in the world of dolls and doll fashions. Back in the 1950's, Deluxe Reading sold a doll kit called Candy Fashions that included an 18in (46cm) fashion doll named Candy. The kit included Candy's ensembles along with the accessories and three mannequins on which to display them. The mannequins were essentially the doll's body minus the head, arms and legs with a wooden rod up the middle. The mannequins were then set on a round stand. It was a great concept for the time, but the mannequins were very large and needed a lot of space to display the other fashions that came with the doll. These dolls were usually sold in grocery stores, and quite a few can be found in mint condition today.

The 1960's were the Barbie® doll era. She was all the rage with her miniature fashions. Young girls loved this 3D paper doll that they could actually hold in their hands and dress without the outfits slipping off. Barbie®, in a sense, was a miniature mannequin in that young girls loved to display her on dressers, shelves, and nightstands dressed in all her finery. Pattern companies even created patterns explicitly for her so that mothers could sew the latest design for their daughters. The Mattel Toy Company even developed a miniature cardboard fashion salon complete with cardboard mannequins to stand in the window and display Barbie's® wonderful haute couture. Girls could make believe that they were the proprietors of a French fashion salon and were showing the latest Paris couture.

Then came the Dawn® doll and all her friends in the 1970's. Along with her hip fashions came a small gold mannequin to display all her groovy cloths. You could dress her in your favorite outfit of the time and display the rest with minimal space since she was only 6-1/2in (17cm) tall. The 70's also gave us the Marie Osmond sewing mannequins which were 19in (48cm) tall. She came with her own patterns and booklet.

A 15-1/2in (39cm) fashion doll hit the scene in the 1990's. Her name was Gene Marshall. She was created by Mel Odom and produced by Ashton

Mannequins to display the outfits from the Candy Doll by Delux Reading.

A Marie Osmond mannequin doll with patterns from the 1970's.

Drake. She gave us another way to look at dolls and fashion. She was easier to dress than the Barbie® doll, which is much smaller in comparison and her fashions were fabulous. Ashton Drake brought out the Gene mannequin in 1997 as a means of displaying her wonderful fashions. That way you didn't have to store all those beautiful fashions away. Later in the decade, the Robert Tonner Doll Company created Tyler Wentworth a new 16in (41cm) fashion doll with wonderful contemporary fashions. Robert told me that he listened to the collectors when they asked him to produce patterns for Tyler. He also decided that if he was going to make the patterns, he should have a seamstress mannequin to fit the fashions as well. He wanted it to be just like a real seamstress mannequin that you could use pins on, and it would have Tyler's measurements. Therefore, he made it out of foam rubber, covered it with material, and added the metal stand.

Another great mannequin came out in 1999 when the Knickerbocker Company's Daisy and Willow dolls got their own full-body mannequin for displaying their fashions. She also came with two sets of arms for posing diversity. People love this concept because it cost less than the dolls and you could display all of their hip clothing along with the actual dolls. Many people have told me that they collect certain dolls because they love the fashions, and they say they use the dolls as mannequins for displaying the fashions. I myself am one of those collectors. If I see a doll with beautiful well-made fashions, I will get one doll and usually as many of the fashions as possible. However, then I have to buy more of the dolls to be able to display more of the fashions—it's a vicious cycle from which I find no escape (thankfully). I think that more doll companies may decide in the future that including miniature mannequins to display their doll's fashions is a good idea.

The talented team of David Escobedo and Brian Shafer, also known as DAE in the fashion doll world, are developing another mannequin. It is being called a "miniquin". It is more of a bust and a hand that is painted. Then a wig is applies so that it can display miniature hats, jewelry, and accessories. I have used an unpainted one to display jewelry and accessories that go with the outfits that I have designed for my company. These "miniquins" are very fashionable looking. These are just few examples.

This Simply Gene platinum doll with three mannequins in the background.

This is a DAE Miniquin front view.

Here is a profile of the DAE Miniquin.

This back view of the DAE Miniquin shows the intricate beading on her hat.

Right: This front view shows another Miniquin.

Below: This profile of the DAE Miniquin shows off her beaded earrings.

Below Right: The back view of the DAE Miniquin.

Left: Here is another 1950's Miniquin dressed in the latest fashion accessories.

Below Left: What a great profile this Miniquin has.

Below: The back view of this Miniquin shows her stylish haircut under an equally stylish hat.

This very daring Miniquin wears stylish makeup and retro accessories.

The profile shows the gorgeous hat and retro jewelry.

Here is the back view of this brilliant fashion.

These miniature mannequins create a miniature window display.

These miniature mannequins are used to display a 16in (41cm) doll fashion.

This Daisy and Willow mannequin shows off in her blue evening gown.

Here she is in some lingerie.

Price Guide

Mannequin Dolls Price Guide

All prices are for mint condition mannequins and kits. Prices will vary depending on condition of mannequins and kits. Prices may also vary from coast to coast or from region to region. Prices derived were gathered from several sources and not just from the author. The author is not responsible for accuracy of prices, nor is the publisher. Page numbers will be given after the pattern description when a picture of the mannequin or kit is shown in the book, otherwise no page number will be given.

Butterick Mannequin Sewing Kits				
		Year	**Value**	**Page**
Junior Miss Mannequin	Set included a 12-1/2in (32cm) mannequin and three patterns and material.	1949	$250	43
Sew Easy Designing Set	Set included a 12-1/2in (32cm) mannequin and six patterns and accessories.	1949	$225	40

McCalls Mannequin Sewing Kit				
		Year	**Value**	**Page**
Peggy the Modern Fashion Model	Set included a 12-1/2in (32cm) mannequin doll and three patterns and accessories.	1949	$350	46
Peggy the Modern Fashion Model	Set included a 12-1/2in (32cm) mannequin doll, one pattern, and instructions.	1949	$200	48

Simplicity Mannequin Sewing Kit Latexture Products Inc.				
		Year	Value	Page
Miniature Fashions Sewing Kit	Set included a 12-1/2in (32cm) mannequin and four patterns.	1949	$250	50
Marianne's Fashion Designing Set	Set included a 12-1/2in (32cm) mannequin and three patterns.	1949	$300	52
Suzanne the Mannequin	Set included a 15in (38cm) mannequin and three patterns.	1949	$200	55
Suzanne the Mannequin	Set included a 15in (38cm) mannequin and three patterns, accessories and half mannequin with stand.	1949	$350	56

Singer Mannequin Sewing Kit				
		Year	Value	Page
The Singer Mannequin Doll Set	Set included a 12-1/2in (32cm) mannequin doll, six patterns and accessories.	1949	$250	60
The Singer Mannequin Doll Set	Set included a 12-1/2in (32cm) mannequin doll, six patterns, miniature Singer sewing machine, and accessories.	1949	$400	Not shown

Off-Brand Mannequin Sewing Kits				
		Year	Value	Page
Little Traveler Sewing Kit	Set included a 10in (25cm) mannequin doll, patterns, scissors, material, thread, needles, and felt hats.	1940's	$75	64
Little Traveler Sewing Kit	Set included a 6in (15cm) mannequin doll, patterns, material, scissors, thread, and needles.	1940's	$65	69

Off-Brand Mannequin Sewing Kits (continued)				
		Year	Value	Page
Jean Darling Sewing Outfit	Set included a 6in (15cm) bisque mannequin doll, 6 dresses, 3 pots with flowers, thread, needles, thimbles, scissors, and 3 small spools of thread.	1936	$80	Not shown
Jean Darling Luggage Doll Sewing Kit	Set included a 7in (18cm) mannequin doll with all the cutout clothing, thread, needles and scissors.	1949	$65	Not shown
Mary Lou Doll Mannequin	Set included a 9in (23cm) vinyl mannequin doll, directions for putting the outfits together, and the dresses that you had to cut out and fit on the doll.	1950's	$85	74
Collette Doll Mannequin	Set included a 9in (23cm) vinyl mannequin doll, directions for putting the outfits together, and the dresses that you had to cut out and fit on the doll.	1950's	$85	71
Lingerie Lou Mannequin Doll	Set included a 5in (13cm) vinyl mannequin doll, directions and pattern.	1952	$20	76
Joan the Paper Mannequin Doll	Set included a 5in (13cm) paper mannequin doll, fashion guide, punch out dress patterns, and material for dresses.	1950's	$20	78
Belinda the Mannequin Doll	Set included 12in (31cm) mannequin doll, material, scissors, and patterns.	1940's	$40	73

Pattern Prices for the Sewing Mannequins

All prices are for mint condition unused patterns. Prices will vary depending on condition of patterns. Prices may also vary from coast to coast or from region to region. Prices derived were gathered from several sources and not just from the author. The author is not responsible for accuracy of prices, nor is the publisher. Page numbers will be given after the pattern description when a picture of the pattern is shown in the book, otherwise no page number will be given.

McCall Mannequin Patterns						
				Year	Value	Page
# 1058	12-1/2in (32cm)	Mannequin Doll		1949	$55	91
# 6600-1	12-1/2in (32cm)	Mannequin Doll	Nurses Uniform	1949	$45	90
# 6600-2	12-1/2in (32cm)	Mannequin Doll	Princess Dress	1949	$35	90
# 6600-3	12-1/2in (32cm)	Mannequin Doll	Daytime or Date Dress	1949	$45	91
Simplicity Mannequin Patterns						
				Year	Value	Page
# 4359	12-1/2in (32cm)	Mannequin Doll	Dress with Sailor Collar	1949	$25	99
# 4387	12-1/2in (32cm)	Mannequin Doll	Dress with Ribbons	1949	$25	99
# 4401	12-1/2in (32cm)	Mannequin Doll	Day Dress with Button Front	1949	$25	52
# 4496	12-1/2in (32cm)	Mannequin Doll	Apron	1949	$25	98
# 4710	12-1/2in (32cm)	Mannequin Doll	Day Dress with Flower	1949	$25	99
# 4965	12-1/2in (32cm)	Mannequin Doll	Day Dress with Square neck	1949	$25	98
# 4977	12-1/2in (32cm)	Mannequin Doll	Day Dress	1949	$25	98
# 4065	15in (38cm)	Mannequin Doll	Long Evening Dress	1949	$35	101
# 4390	15in (38cm)	Mannequin Doll	Day Dress with Pockets and belt	1949	$35	100
# 4394	15in (38cm)	Mannequin Doll	Dress with Pockets	1949	$35	101
# 4402	15in (38cm)	Mannequin Doll	Blouse and Long Skirt	1949	$35	57
# 4411	15in (38cm)	Mannequin Doll	Tailored Suit	1949	$35	N/A
# 4805	15in (38cm)	Mannequin Doll	Evening Dress	1949	$35	N/A
# 4938	15in (38cm)	Mannequin Doll	Full Apron	1949	$35	101
# 4980	15in (38cm)	Mannequin Doll	Dress with tie belt	1949	$35	100
# 4981	15in (38cm)	Mannequin Doll	Blouse and Shorts	1949	$35	100
# 4984	15in (38cm)	Mannequin Doll	Dress with belt	1949	$35	101
# 4995	15in (38cm)	Mannequin Doll	Long Slip	1949	$35	100

Butterick Mannequin Patterns	Year	Value	Page
Set No. One Drindle Dress, Party Dress, Bridal Gown 12-1/2in (32cm) Mannequin Doll	1949	$45	94
Set No. Eight Included # 5979, # 6083, and #5917 12-1/2in (32cm) Mannequin Doll	1949	$65	42
Set No. Nine Included # 6057, # 5744, and # 6015 12-1/2in (32cm) Mannequin Doll	1949	$65	42
Set No. One Included # 5366, # 5100, and # 5354 12-1/2in (32cm) Mannequin Doll	1949	$65	59
Set No. Two Included # 5460 or 5453, #5428, and # 5547 or 5453 12-1/2in (32cm) Mannequin Doll	1949	$65	59
Fashion Craft Designing Set No. One Drindle Dress, Party Dress, Nurses Uniform 12in (31cm) Mannequin Doll	1942	$65	93

Helen Huntington Jones Mannequin Patterns		Year	Value	Page
17th Century	12-1/2in (32cm) Mannequin Doll	1949	$15	103
American Revolution	12-1/2in (32cm) Mannequin Doll	1949	$15	103
Early Nineteenth Century	12-1/2in (32cm) Mannequin Doll	1949	$15	102
Civil War Period	12-1/2in (32cm) Mannequin Doll	1949	$15	102
Belinda's Nautical Princess Dress, Tailored Suit, and Afternoon Dress	12-1/2in (32cm) Mannequin Doll	1949	$15	73

Lingerie Lou Mannequin Patterns				
Country	Set No.	Year	Value	Page
Spanish	# 102	1952	$5	77
Italian	# 103	1952	$5	N/A
German	# 104	1952	$5	77
Swedish	# 111	1952	$5	77
Dutch	# 113	1952	$5	77
Polish	# 114	1952	$5	77
Denmark	# 117	1952	$5	N/A
Russian	# 118	1952	$5	N/A
Gypsy	# 119	1952	$5	N/A
South America	# 120	1952	$5	N/A
Austrian	# 124S	1952	$5	N/A
Israeli	# 126S	1952	$5	N/A
Hindu	# 127S	1952	$5	N/A
Japanese	# 128S	1952	$5	N/A

Marianne's Mannequin Patterns						
				Year	Value	Page
# 101	12-1/2in (32cm)	Mannequin Doll	Easy-to-Make Dress	1949	$25	97
# 102	12-1/2in (32cm)	Mannequin Doll	Nurse's Uniform	1949	$25	97
# 103	12-1/2in (32cm)	Mannequin Doll	Day Time Dress	1949	$25	97

Suzanne's Mannequin Patterns						
				Year	Value	Page
# 303	12-1/2in (32cm)	Mannequin Doll	Easy-to-Make Dress	1949	$25	95
#2001	12-1/2in (32cm)	Mannequin Doll	Daytime Dress	1942	$35	96
#2002	12-1/2in (32cm)	Mannequin Doll	Nurses Uniform	1942	$35	96
#2004	12-1/2in (32cm)	Mannequin Doll	Nurses Cape	1942	$35	96

About the Author

Doris was born in Los Angeles, California in 1951 and has lived in California all her life. She graduated from Mojave High School, in Mojave, California, in 1970 and later moved to Corona, California where she met and married her husband, Robert. They have two daughters, Christina 28, a flight attendant, and Leah 18, a senior in high school, and several dogs.

She attended Riverside Community College and graduated in 1994 with distinction in computer information systems. She says attending college gave her the self-esteem and determination she needed to start a business of her own five years ago. Doris has been collecting dolls for the past 25 years and currently has about 1,000 various fashion dolls. She loves the fashion over the doll, and believes that the doll is just a mannequin waiting to be dressed.

Doris has written articles for several magazines including *Miller's* fashion doll magazine and *Doll Reader* magazine. She also does freelance doll designs for Paradise Galleries in San Diego. One of her designs was recently used on a Patricia Rose groom doll. Doris' design work has been recognized and featured in *Riverside Press Enterprise*, *Miller's* fashion doll magazine, and in Jim Faraone's *2nd Fashion Doll Makeovers: Learn From the Artists*. Doris has won several awards for her designs and was the promoter of two Fashion Doll Conventions for the Make-A-Wish foundation, which raised $20,000 for that wonderful organization.

Doris owns Fashion Boulevard, a new and upcoming fashion-doll company, that manufactures couture fashion for the 15-1/2in – 16in (39cm – 41cm) fashion dolls, and hopefully will soon have a new 16in (41cm) fashion doll of her own on the market. This has been a dream of hers from the time she started designing her own fashions. You can visit her business site at www.Fashion-Boulevard.com.